SUCCESS-FOCUSED MENTALITY :
The Step-by-Step Guide to Rewiring
Your Brain to Achieve Success in Life

By
Charles C. Vanwinkle

TABLE OF CONTENTS

CHAPTER 1

CHAPTER 2

CHAPTER 3

CHAPTER 4

CHAPTER 5

CHAPTER 6

CHAPTER 7

CHAPTER 8

CHAPTER 1

<u>*The Key to Being Successful*</u>

The foundation of success is based on a combination of important concepts and activities that lead people or organizations to accomplish their objectives, meet their ambitions, and produce good results. The foundation of success is built upon a combination of essential principles and actions that lead to positive outcomes.

Success may be understood in a variety of ways, depending on the circumstances and the individual's views; yet, certain fundamental components are necessary for its achievement.

Clear Vision and Goal:
Having a distinct idea of what it is you want to accomplish, together with

your goals, is the first step towards achieving success. This vision should be backed by SMART objectives; that is, they should be precise, measurable, attainable, relevant, and time-bound. Having a clear idea of where you want to go makes it easier to maintain concentration and motivation.

Passion and Purpose:
Genuine enthusiasm and a clear understanding of one's place in the world are two of the most potent driving factors that may drive one's tenacity and endurance. When you are enthusiastic about what you do, it is much simpler to push through challenges and maintain your dedication to the route you have chosen.

Continuous Education and Adaptability: Adopting a "growth mindset" and maintaining an attitude that is receptive to new information is essential to achieving one's goals. Because of this, people and organizations that are successful must be able to adapt and advance along with the changing environment. They are open to gaining new skills, maintaining their natural curiosity, and welcoming innovation.

Hard Work and Diligence:
The achievement of goals is rarely possible without the application of significant effort. A solid work ethic, together with diligence and discipline, is very necessary. Consistent effort and the mental fortitude to persevere

in the face of adversity are two of the most important factors that contribute to long-term success.

Resilience and perseverance:
Resilience and perseverance are essential traits to have on any path to achievement since there will inevitably be obstacles and challenges along the way. The capacity to recover quickly from adversity and go on with one's life despite it is a key component of resilience. Your ability to persevere enables you to keep your eye on the prize despite the challenges and setbacks you encounter along the way.

Integrity and ethics: A success that is founded on unethical practices or dishonesty may result in short-term rewards, but it may lead to long-term implications that are not favorable. Honesty, integrity, and ethical conduct are the cornerstones around which genuine achievement should be built.

Emotional Intelligence:
Emotional Intelligence refers to a person's capacity to comprehend and control their feelings as well as those of themselves and others. It is a skill that is very useful in the pursuit of success. Emotional intelligence is beneficial to the development of solid relationships, the promotion of effective communication, and the enhancement of collaborative efforts.

Networking and collaboration:

Networking and collaboration are essential components of success since most endeavors need the participation of several people. Creating a solid network of encouraging people who have your back and working together with those who share your values may lead to the discovery of exciting new possibilities and add depth to your experience.

Time management and prioritization: Successful people are those that place a high value on their own time and can prioritize their responsibilities properly. They have a plan for everything, and they concentrate on actions that get them closer to achieving their objectives.

Adopting a Positive Mindset:
It is possible to make a considerable improvement in one's circumstances by retaining a positive mindset, even when confronted with difficult circumstances. Creativity, problem-solving skills, and resiliency may all be fostered by cultivating a positive attitude.

Management of funds:
If you want to be successful in your company or your personal life, you need to be able to manage your funds wisely. Having a solid grasp of one's finances via the use of tools such as budgeting, investments, and planning may assist preserve stability and open the door to expansion.

Going Back and Gratitude:

Giving Back to Society and Showing Gratitude Successful people often understand the significance of giving back to society and showing gratitude for the accomplishments they have attained. Giving back to causes that a person cares about may provide them with a feeling of purpose and fulfillment that goes beyond their achievements.

Keep in mind that the way to achieve success varies from person to person and organization to organization. It takes dedication, tenacity, and the desire to learn from both triumphs and mistakes to do it. Developing a firm foundation that is built on these principles will help you find fulfillment in your path and get you closer to accomplishing the objectives you have set for yourself.

<u>Determining What Success Means to You; What does success mean to you?</u>

The term "success" is notoriously open to interpretation and may mean many different things to different people. It is not just about acquiring fortune, fame, or the acknowledgment of one's peers in society. Rather, it is a very personal and comprehensive idea that embraces a broad range of accomplishments and accomplishments in a variety of areas of one's life.

To me, success entails the following:

- *Finding contentment and delight in the occupations and activities that offer significance and satisfaction to one's life is one definition of the path to fulfillment and happiness.*

- *Having a distinct understanding of one's life's purpose and coordinating one's activities with one's core beliefs and areas of interest are the hallmarks of a purposeful life.*

- *Adopting a learning and personal development mindset to continuously grow one's capabilities, body of information, and viewpoints.*

- *Contributing to the happiness of other people and the world as a whole while also making a positive imprint on the lives of those who are closest to me is what I mean when I talk about having a positive impact.*

- *The capacity to navigate problems with fortitude and adjust to changing circumstances without losing sight of my objectives is an essential aspect of adaptability.*

- *Developing meaningful connections with other people via the cultivation of authentic relationships requires trust, respect, and empathy.*

- *Having a life that is well-balanced means achieving a healthy equilibrium in all aspects of one's life, including work, relationships, leisure, and self-care.*

- *Freedom and Autonomy Consist of having the freedom to make decisions that are congruent with my beliefs and objectives, as well as the autonomy to direct the course of my own life.*

- *Conquering Fear involves not allowing myself to be held back by the fear of failing or being judged, but rather choosing to take measured chances to follow my ambitions.*

- *Being thankful for the opportunities, experiences, and benefits that come one's way is an essential component of gratitude.*

Recognizing that success is not a destination but rather a never-ending journey is one of the most important things that one can do. It requires introspection, self-awareness, and a grasp of the factors that genuinely contribute to one's sense of accomplishment.

When success is conceptualized in a manner that is both all-encompassing and unique to the person, achieving it is transformed into a more significant endeavor, one that transcends the expectations of society, and that ultimately results in a life that is both more fulfilling and more meaningful.

<u>The Value of Believing in Oneself and Exuding Confidence</u>

The importance of having self-confidence is beyond anything that you could ever comprehend. It has the potential to improve all aspects of your life. While a lack of self-assurance can have a detrimental impact on your social relationships, profession, accomplishments, and even your mood, it will also prevent you from reaching your full potential.

How would you define self-confidence?

To have confidence is essentially the same thing as to trust. When you say that you trust someone or that you have complete faith in them, what you really mean is that you believe in them.

In a similar vein, having self-confidence is having faith in both oneself and one's talents. It means having confidence in oneself and being able to be at ease with one's authentic self. A positive mental attitude towards one's capabilities and strengths is the foundation of self-confidence.

A lack of self-confidence, on the other side, might cause you to be full of self-doubt, be meek or subservient, and have difficulties trusting people. It's possible that you feel worthless, unloved, or too sensitive to criticism.

Your level of self-assurance may be influenced by the circumstances. You could, for instance, have a lot of self-assurance when it comes to your academic performance, but struggle with self-assurance when it comes to your interpersonal interactions.

The distinctions between having self-confidence and having excessive amounts of it

People often get self-assurance and confidence confused with being overconfident in their abilities. As was said before, having confidence in one's skills implies having faith in one's abilities, but having overconfidence in one's abilities involves overestimating one's genuine talents.

One fundamental distinction between the two categories is that an overconfident person has an unwavering belief in himself, to the point that they don't even consider the possibility that anything may go wrong. Confidence, on the other hand, involves having faith in one's talents while acknowledging the possibility of making errors.

Why is it so crucial to have self-confidence?

A person's level of self-confidence not only has a significant effect on a variety of facets of their existence but also on the more minute details of how they go about their everyday lives. The following are some of the many benefits of having self-confidence:

1. It helps one have a higher opinion of themselves.
Believing in both one's capabilities and the value that one brings to the world are essential components of healthy self-esteem. Having confidence in oneself is a doorway to gaining stronger self-esteem, and vice versa. Having self-esteem also contributes to having confidence in oneself. People who have healthy self-esteem are better able to deal with the trials and tribulations of life, learn to cultivate happiness and love in their lives and experience mental serenity.

2. Reduces feelings of anxiousness.

Having confidence in oneself is one technique to lessen the amount of worry and dread that exists in a person's life. A person's lack of self-confidence may be traced back to the origin of almost all of the problems that are associated with social anxiety, poor self-esteem, and certain other types of anxiety. A lack of self-confidence causes a person to want to avoid any circumstance in which they would be forced to be the center of attention, which only serves to reinforce their nervous behavior.

3. a healthy sense of self-worth.
The significance of having self-confidence is directly proportional to the degree to which a person feels at ease in their skin. People who are secure in themselves

are aware that acknowledging their shortcomings does not lower their sense of value. When one is self-assured and believes that they are capable of overcoming their shortcomings in the future, it is much simpler to accept the shortcomings that they now have.

4. Helps one become a more effective leader.
Self-confidence is one of the attributes that make a successful leader, and it's essential. A leader is someone who is not only able to communicate clearly and assuredly but also has a compelling personality.

5. Boosts one's level of motivation.
When you have confidence, you will naturally feel more motivated to do

those activities, as opposed to someone who has low confidence and may not feel as motivated to complete such chores. People who lack confidence tend to be consumed with the worry that they will fail at something.

6. Causes joy and satisfaction.
A self-assured individual does not hold back from engaging in any activity in their life. There are no self-blaming or brooding thoughts, and there are no regrets over possibilities that were missed. The absence of regret in one's life naturally results in a happier existence than the norm would otherwise dictate.

7.   *Improved   interpersonal connections.*

Self-assured people don't waste mental energy worrying about how others will see them in any given social situation, and as a result, their relationships with others are more open and sincere. Confident people are thought to have better relationships than those who lack confidence since honesty is a trait that contributes to the improvement of relationships.

The following are some ways you may boost your self-confidence:

Everyone wants to raise their level of self-confidence so that they may perform better now that they understand the significance of having self-confidence in everyday life. What are the several routes that one may use to accomplish it?

1. *Acceptance: the first step in any endeavor to reform or improve anything is to acknowledge the shortcomings and mistakes. Recognize that your personality features include a lack of self-confidence to some degree.*

2. *Identification: It involves making an objective inventory of all of the positive and negative aspects of your personality. In addition to this, make use of the skills and abilities you possess that are applicable. Reward and congratulate yourself for the work you've been making and*

the accomplishments you've made.

3. Take away all of the negative thoughts: Clear your head of any unfavorable ideas you have about yourself. Your road towards greater self-confidence will be significantly hampered by the presence of such negative thoughts and feelings.

4. Kindness and compassion towards oneself are required whenever you come up against a challenge. Don't wallow in your past mistakes.

5. Establish objectives that are both attainable and realistic: It is unrealistic to anticipate

perfection since it is impossible to achieve perfection in every facet of one's life.

6. *Be assertive: We need to acquire the skills necessary to learn how to be aggressive without coming off as rude. People who are more confident than their competitors often come out on top, even if they lack the necessary abilities. This is because their self-assurance enables them to persuade others to side with them, rather than depending on their abilities to convince people to see things differently.*

7. *When you are experiencing strong feelings, take some time*

to calm down and think rationally about the issue.

8. *It's important to avoid jumping to conclusions about yourself, other people, and the world around you.*

9. *Realize that your future is not predetermined by the terrible life events you have had in the past.*

10. *Master the art of politely declining ridiculous demands.*

11. *If you feel like you need more assistance, individual counseling may be able to assist you in being more self-assured.*

Developing a Mindset That Is
Both Upbeat and Optimistic
Regarding Future Progress

The cultivation of a growth-oriented mentality is a potent strategy to promote personal development, increase resiliency, and achieve success in a variety of facets of life.

The following are some methods that may assist you in cultivating such a mindset:

1. Permit yourself to fantasize about things.
A dream is the starting point for each new endeavor or accomplishment. Don't put any boundaries or restrictions on your dreams; just let yourself daydream. If you accept your aspirations as a part of who you are

as a creative person, you will be able to see fresh chances for personal development. Now put them to the test.

2. Recognise and accept the existence of your flaws.
Hiding from your shortcomings and failings is a foolproof technique to ensure that you will never be able to overcome them. Your efforts to establish a development mentality will also be hampered as a result of this. If you accept and love your flaws, you may break the power that they have over your attitude and achieve success despite those flaws.

3. Experiment with something new every day.

If you make it a goal to try something new each day of the year, at the end of the year you will have experienced 365 different things for the first time. The likelihood of stumbling into something that you are strong at, something that you like, or both is significantly increased.

You will quickly create a personal development mentality in which you perceive challenges rather than problems and are unafraid to attempt new things. This is by far the most essential benefit of developing a growth mindset.

4. Be your own biggest fan and supporter.
If you want to succeed at anything new, you need to be your cheerleader.

Create a routine of praising and motivating yourself by engaging in positive self-talk.

Keep in mind how fantastic it will feel after you have mastered the new talent you are working on. Consider how you would support a friend or coworker if they were beginning a new learning experience, and then coach yourself in a manner that is analogous to how you would encourage them.

5. Develop a sense of direction in your life.
When you begin to cultivate a growth mindset, one of the first things you will notice is that you are beginning to have a higher sense of purpose. Always keep in mind the bigger

vision, as this will make it easier for you to keep moving forward.

6. Interact with fresh and different individuals.
Acquaint yourself with individuals and communities that you may not have spent much time with in the past and engage in dialogue with them.

If you go into these dialogues with an open mind, you will not only pick up new information but also have your current beliefs called into question. Your imagination and spirit of exploration will both get a boost as a result of this.

7. Have confidence in your skills and abilities.

Make a pact with yourself to always believe in your capacity to grow and adapt to new circumstances.

Take precautions to avoid allowing the unfavorable opinions of others to distract you or sap your motivation. Even while feedback in the form of constructive criticism is always beneficial, it is essential to find your voice and pay attention to it. Examine the source of the criticism and determine if it is coming from a place of progress or a stagnant worldview.

8. Place more value on progress than on quickness
It is important to keep in mind that you are working towards developing

a development mentality, rather than a "quick fix" attitude.

This is a never-ending process in which you never stop learning and expanding your knowledge. This is not a race; rather, it is a marathon. Don't give up if it takes you some time to master some of the new abilities and behaviors you're learning. Adjust to your rate of progress.

9. Pay more attention to the journey than to the destination.
There are probably certain pursuits that you have not engaged in because you do not have faith that you would be successful at them. Ask yourself, "Does it matter if I am not very good at it?" and genuinely think about the answer.

The correct response is "No." If you are doing something because you like it, the skill level is not as important. You will have a lot more fun and you could, without even realizing it, uncover something that you are genuinely excellent at if you put more of your attention on the experience rather than the consequence of that experience.

10. Recognise that you are responsible for your attitude.
Once you've developed a growth mentality, you should take ownership of it. Recognize that you are someone who has a development mindset, and be glad to allow that attitude to lead you for the whole of your professional life.

It is important to keep in mind that the process of developing a growth-oriented and optimistic mentality is a continuous one.

Exercise self-compassion and be patient with yourself to go forward. You may cultivate a mentality that gives you the ability to overcome obstacles, grasp opportunities, and lead a life that is more satisfying if you give it time, effort, and attention consistently over some time.

CHAPTER 2

<u>Setting Objectives and Having a Vision for the Future</u>

Defining your goals and having a distinct plan on how to achieve them are two of the most important factors in attaining both professional and personal success. They serve as a guide, a source of inspiration, and a compass for navigating the journey from dream to reality.

Creating a vision and creating goals may be broken down as follows:

1. Setting Objectives:
The process of creating goals includes identifying objectives in a manner that is precise, measurable, attainable, relevant, and time-bound (often abbreviated as SMART). It aids

in the process of breaking down the larger goal into more manageable, achievable tasks that can be accomplished more quickly. The following is a good strategy for creating goals for yourself:

- *Specified: Clearly explain your objectives in a way that is specific and free of ambiguity. You need to be very explicit about what it is you want to accomplish.*

- *Measurable: Create a set of criteria that will allow you to track your progress and provide a benchmark for when the objective has been accomplished.*

- *Set objectives that are attainable by keeping in mind your current skills and resources. Setting objectives that are impossible to achieve might result in frustration and disappointment, even though it is beneficial to have lofty aspirations.*

- *Important: Check to see if your aims and your overall vision and values are compatible with one another. They should have significance for you and be pertinent to the goal you have set for your life.*

- *Time-bound: To instill a feeling of urgency, it is helpful to give each objective a specific due date.*

This will also assist you in being focused and responsible.

2. Vision:
A long-term, all-encompassing concept or image of what you aim to accomplish in your life or a particular area of your life is referred to as a vision. It acts like a lighthouse, illuminating the path ahead and pointing you in the right way.

When you are developing your vision, keep the following in mind:

- *Picture the greatest Possible result for Yourself and Don't Be scared to Dream Big: Don't be scared to dream big and picture the greatest possible result for yourself. Your vision needs to be something that motivates and excites you.*

- *Ensure that your vision is linked with your core values and the things that are important to you. Make sure that your vision is consistent with your basic values. It ought to be a reflection of who you are and the values that you uphold.*

- *Visualization is imagining your ideal future using specific details and feelings in your mind's eye. Your vision will become more appealing and attainable as a result of this.*

- *Adaptability: Even while a vision might point you on the right* path, you should be willing to modify it as necessary in response to shifting conditions or emerging understandings and experiences.

- *Positive and Empowering: Your vision should make you feel good and provide you the ability to make it a reality by taking action. It should be something that you have a strong desire to do and are enthusiastic about pursuing.*

Bringing Together the Process of Goal-Setting and Vision:

Your vision should operate as a beacon that points you in the right direction in general, and your objectives should serve as the stepping *stones that help you get there. Every objective you pursue ought to be congruent with your vision and should work towards bringing it into being step by step.*

You should routinely evaluate your progress, make any necessary changes to your objectives, and maintain your dedication to the greater vision. Celebrate your successes along the road, but don't forget that failures are an inevitable part of the path you're on.

When you combine the process of goal setting with the formulation of a distinct vision, you build a robust foundation for your own personal development, accomplishment, and living a life motivated by purpose.

The Skill Behind Establishing SMART Goals

It is a strong and effective strategy to guarantee that your objectives are well-defined, attainable, and actionable if you set them using the S.M.A.R.T. methodology. Specific, Measurable, Achievable, Relevant, and Time-bound are the five components that make up the S.M.A.R.T. framework. A deeper look at each component of defining goals using the S.M.A.R.T. method is as follows:

1. Specific:
Think carefully and deliberately about the goals you wish to achieve. Stay away from objectives that are too broad and instead concentrate on

pinpointing precisely what it is you want to accomplish. Put yourself in your shoes and ask the "W" questions: What do I want to achieve? Why is it necessary to do so? Which parties are involved? Where exactly will it take place? Which resources are going to be necessary?

A particular aim may be anything along the lines of, "I want to lose 10 pounds by following a healthy diet and exercising regularly."

2. Measurable:
Establish concrete criteria so that you can monitor your progress and know when you have accomplished your objective. You may keep yourself motivated by objectively evaluating your performance, which is made

possible when you have objectives that can be measured.

An example of a measurable objective is "I will keep a log of my weekly weight and the number of calories I consume each day so that I can monitor my progress towards shedding 10 pounds."

3. Achievable:
Establish objectives for yourself that are attainable and in line with your skills. Setting objectives that are extremely ambitious and that are above your present ability may lead to dissatisfaction and demotivation, even though it is admirable to strive for the stars.

An example of a goal that can be achieved is "I will aim to lose 1-2 pounds per week through a balanced diet and regular exercise, which is considered a healthy and attainable rate of weight loss." This is an example of a goal that can be achieved.

4. Relevant:
Make sure that your values, desires, and overall vision are all in line with the goals that you have set for yourself. The objective needs to have some significance and be relevant to the larger purpose of your life.

A relevant goal might be something along the lines of, "Losing weight is important to me because it will improve my overall health, boost my *self-confidence, and allow me to engage in activities that I enjoy."*

5. Time-bound:
Establish a concrete timetable for accomplishing your objective. The presence of a deadline instills a feeling of imminence and makes it easier to maintain concentration and dedication to carrying out the plan of action.

An example of a goal that is time-bound might be "I will lose 10 pounds within the next 10 weeks, starting today."

With the help of the S.M.A.R.T. framework, you may turn hazy concepts into well-defined objectives that can be carried out. This strategy improves your chances of success by giving you clarity, motivation, and a well-defined path to follow to reach your goals. Keep in mind that you should routinely examine your progress, make any necessary adjustments to your objectives, and celebrate your accomplishments along the way.

Developing an Inspiring Goal or Mission Statement for Your Life and Career

You may identify what it is that you want to accomplish in life and how you want to live by going through the process of self-discovery and reflection that is involved in the creation of a compelling vision for your life and work.

The following are some methods that can assist you in developing a compelling vision:

1. Self-Reflection:
Spend some time thinking about the things that are important to you, such as your interests, values, strengths, and ambitions. Think about the things you do that give you a sense of accomplishment, as well as the aspects of your life in which you'd want to see more development and progress.

2. Dare to Dream:
Permit oneself to imagine without any restrictions. Imagine that you had access to all of the resources and possibilities in the world. Describe what a perfect life and job would look

like for you. Let's get rid of the limitations you've put on yourself and try to imagine bigger than your present situation.

3. Determine Your Core Values:
Bring more clarity to your fundamental values, which are the ideas and guiding principles that inform your choices and behaviors. Your vision needs to be consistent with these principles to guarantee that it will provide genuine meaning and purpose to both your life and your work.

4. Establish Detailed Objectives:
Converting your long-term vision into precise, attainable objectives that are in line with your beliefs and ambitions will help you get there faster. Along

the path to achieving your compelling vision, these objectives will act as checkpoints to mark your progress.

5. Visualization:
Utilize skills of visualization to help you psychologically immerse yourself in the alluring image you have. Imagine that you have already achieved all of your professional aspirations and are living the life of your dreams. Developing a powerful emotional connection to your goal and boosting your drive may be accomplished by using visualization.

6. Put it in writing:
Write out what you want to accomplish and put it into words. Describe in vivid detail your ideal life and career, including the

accomplishments you have had, the experiences you have had, and the influence you intend to create.

7. Make a Vision Board for Yourself:
Your inspiring idea might be physically represented on a board known as a vision board. Make a collage that you may look at daily to remind yourself of your vision by collecting pictures, phrases, and symbols that are significant to your objectives and objectives for the future.

8. Try to Get Some Responses and Support:
Talk to someone you can trust, such as close friends, members of your family, or experienced adults. They can provide insightful comments and

assistance, both of which may assist you in honing your vision and remaining on course.

9. Proceed to Act:
A captivating vision may be motivating, but it has to be backed up with action to be effective. Create a plan to achieve your objectives by breaking them down into manageable stages, and then stick to that plan.

10. Keep an open mind:
Life is never predictable, and one's circumstances are always subject to alteration. Maintain an open mind and be willing to alter your perspective if required. The fundamental principles and goals may stay the same, but the approach

used to achieve them may change over time.

11. Examine and Go Over Again:
Examine your vision regularly to make sure it continues to serve your needs and has significance for you. Check-in on both your progress and your objectives every so often and make any modifications.

You will have the ability to follow your interests and make decisions that are purposeful and in line with who you are as a person when you develop a compelling vision for your life and career.

It gives you a feeling of where you are going and why you are doing what you are doing, which makes it easier *for you to maintain your motivation and keep focused on the path that leads to a life that is satisfying and successful.*

Utilizing Your Imagination to Achieve Success and Leveraging the Law of Attraction

The practice of visualizing oneself as achieving a goal is a potent strategy that is often linked to the concept of the Law of Attraction. This is the theory that a person's thoughts can attract either good or bad situations into their lives.

It is necessary to approach the Law of Attraction with a balanced viewpoint and comprehend its limits, even though its popularity has increased in recent years.

You may increase your chances of being successful by successfully using visualization in the following ways:

1. Make Sure Your Goals Are Clear:
It is important to have a firm grasp of your particular objectives before you start visualizing. Determine what success means to you, whether it be in terms of your professional life, the quality of your relationships, your physical well-being, or your personal development.

2. Conjure up a clear image in your mind:
Put your eyes closed and conjure up a clear mental picture of yourself accomplishing your objectives. Utilize each of your senses to the fullest

extent to create the most lifelike mental image possible. Imagine yourself achieving achievement, going through the range of feelings that go along with it, listening to the noises that are happening around you, and being completely present at the moment.

3. Accept and Embrace Happy Emotions:
During the process of visualizing, it is important to concentrate on happy feelings such as happiness, thankfulness, enthusiasm, and self-assurance. Emotions play an important part in the Law of Attraction because they affect the energy that you generate and the energy that you attract.

4. Maintain both your persistence and consistency:

Create a routine out of practicing your visualization skills. Every day, set aside some time just to visualize your accomplishments. Maintaining a consistent approach helps to solidify the mental pictures and emotional sensations linked with your objectives.

5. Visualize the Steps involved, Not Just the Final Result:

While it is important to focus on the outcome, it is also helpful to imagine the stages that will lead to success. Imagine yourself taking action, advancing towards your goals, prevailing over obstacles, and developing as you go along.

6. Utilize Positive Affirmations:
Affirmations of positivity should be included in your visualization. Repeat affirmations that are pertinent to your achievement, such as "I am capable of achieving my goals" or "I attract opportunities that align with my vision."

7. Develop an attitude of gratitude:
During your practice of visualization, make an effort to express thankfulness. A grateful attitude helps cultivate a good outlook, which in turn draws to one more great event.

8. Act in a Way That Inspires You:
However, for it to be effective as a tool for inspiration and concentration, visualization has to be followed by inspired action. Take actionable

measures towards achieving your objectives, and have a proactive mindset while you work towards achieving them.

9. *Maintain an Open Mind Regarding Opportunities:*
Keep an open mind and seize the possibilities that may not have been in your plans. According to the concept of the Law of Attraction, keeping an open mind and maintaining a good attitude may pave the way for synchronicities and happy accidents that are in line with your goals.

10. *Consider the following:*
Visualization is a powerful tool; nevertheless, it is necessary to be realistic about the objectives you set for yourself and the amount of work

that will be needed to attain them. Imagining oneself as successful is not a substitute for putting in long hours of labor, being dedicated, and remaining resilient.

Keep in mind that visualizing your achievement is just one step in the process of obtaining it. It has the potential to improve your attention, drive, and mentality, but it has to be accompanied by action that is grounded in reality as well as a desire to learn and adjust. It is possible to generate a tremendous force that propels you towards achievement by bringing your ideas, feelings, and actions into alignment with your objectives.

CHAPTER 3

Getting Past Obstacles and Difficulties

Conquering difficulties and setbacks is a talent that is essential to obtaining personal development, success, and fulfillment in one's life. You may successfully navigate through challenges and emerge stronger on the other side if you adopt the appropriate mentality and use the appropriate tactics. Life is full of unexpected twists and turns.

The following is a list of strategies that have shown to be useful in overcoming barriers and challenges:

1. _Develop a constructive and upbeat frame of mind by always looking on the bright side._

Instead of obsessing over the bad elements, shift your focus to the chances and possibilities that are presented by the problems. Have faith in your abilities to solve problems and prevail despite the challenges you face.

2. *Acceptance and resiliency: Recognise that adversity is an inevitable component of living a full life. Embrace the difficulties you face as chances for personal development and improvement. You may increase your resilience by reacting positively to challenges and failures, and by doing it with dignity and resolve.*

3. *When confronted with a difficult obstacle, it might be helpful to*

break the problem down into a series of more manageable subtasks. Taking on the procedure one step at a time will make it seem less daunting and will boost the likelihood of your success.

4. *Do Not Be hesitant to Ask for assistance or Seek Support from Friends, Family, Mentors, or coworkers Do not be hesitant to ask for assistance or seek support from friends, family, mentors, or coworkers. Sometimes, gaining a new point of view or being guided in the right direction may bring helpful insights and answers.*

5. *Learn from your mistakes and look at them as stepping stones on the path to success. Examine what you did incorrectly, learn from your mistakes, and use what you've learned to refine your strategy.*

6. *Maintain your flexibility and be open to modifying both your plans and your techniques as necessary. The only thing you can count on in life is change, therefore having the ability to adapt to new situations is essential.*

7. *Imagine yourself reaching your objectives and prevailing over the challenge as you mentally see yourself succeeding. Your*

self-assurance and motivation may both benefit from practicing visualization.

8. *Maintain a Growth mentality. Have the belief that you can improve your skills through consistent effort and devotion. This is the foundation of having a growth mentality. This mentality fosters a never-ending thirst for knowledge and the desire to become better.*

9. *Instead of fixating on the issue at hand, you should make your primary effort to discover a solution to the problem. Look for unique solutions, and don't be afraid to think beyond the box.*

10.

11. *Acknowledge and rejoice in even the little victories along the road as you continue to make progress. Your morale may be boosted and your motivation maintained if you often acknowledge your progress.*

12. *Take care of both your physical and mental health by engaging in the practice of self-care. Participate in pursuits that result in recharging and rejuvenation so that you may tackle difficulties with the vigor you need.*

13. *Maintain Your Dedication: Maintain your dedication to the accomplishment of your objectives and objectives. To*

prevail in the face of adversity, you need both perseverance and resolve.

14. *Learn to Let Go: To go ahead, it is sometimes important to let go of some expectations, beliefs, or attachments to make progress. You must be willing to let go of things that are no longer serving you.*

15. *Maintain your patience, since overcoming challenges may take some time. Have patience, not just with yourself but also with the process.*

16. *Maintain a Grateful Attitude: Make it a habit to be thankful for what you already possess as well*

as the strides you've already made. Being grateful may help you see things in a new light and usher in a state of satisfaction.

Keep in mind that overcoming challenges presents a chance for personal development and advancement. Acknowledge and welcome obstacles as necessary stepping stones on the path to your achievement. You will be able to conquer any challenge that stands in your way if you have a positive outlook, don't give up easily, look for assistance, and be adaptable. If you do these things, you will be able to keep moving forward with grace and dedication toward your objectives.

Recognizing and Overcoming the Limiting Beliefs You Have About Yourself

The key to successful personal development and reaching one's full potential is to become aware of and triumph over limiting ideas held about oneself. These beliefs may be viewed as negative impressions or ideas that we have about ourselves, and they prevent us from achieving our objectives and aspirations.

Identifying and overcoming self-limiting beliefs may be accomplished by the following step-by-step process:

1. Self-Reflection:
Spend some time doing some self-reflection and become more

aware of how your ideas and actions affect you. Pay attention to negative patterns or ideas that keep coming up that keep getting in the way of your success.

2. Put Your Beliefs to the Test:
Investigate the veracity of the ideas you have. Are they predicated on preconceptions or anxieties, or do they take into account genuine facts and actual experiences? Think about how these ideas affect your life and whether or not they are in line with the things that are important to you and the things that you want to accomplish.

3. Investigate the Matter:
Look for data that either confirms or disproves the self-limiting ideas you

already hold. You will often discover that these ideas are not founded on facts but rather on skewed impressions of the world.

4. Replace with positive affirmations: Affirmations of positivity should be used instead of beliefs that are restricting to you. Develop affirmations that will serve as a weapon against your self-limiting beliefs. For instance, change the phrase "I'm not good enough" to "I am capable and deserving of success."

5. Imagine yourself succeeding: Imagine accomplishing your objectives and prevailing over challenges by using the technique of visualization. Participate with as many of your senses as well as your emotions to get the most out of the visualization.

6. Put Yourself Up Against Your Inner Critic:
The voice that encourages limiting thoughts about oneself is known as the inner critic. Confront this critical voice and work on developing self-compassion. You should show yourself the same consideration and encouragement that you would give to a close friend.

7. Put yourself in a positive environment:
Put yourself in situations where you are exposed to good influences and individuals who are supportive of you and believe in your skills. Reduce your time spent in environments that are

negative and perpetuate feelings of inadequacy.

8. *Rejoice in Your Victories:*
Recognize and honor even the smallest of your accomplishments by celebrating them. The positive views you have about yourself are strengthened when you acknowledge and acknowledge your accomplishments.

9. *Adopt a Mindset Focused on Growth:*
Adopt a growth mentality, which is thinking that your capabilities can be improved via the application of work and the acquisition of knowledge. Embrace difficulties as chances for personal development.

10. You Should Act Despite Your Fear:
Beliefs that restrict oneself in some way are often strengthened by fear. Take action even though you are scared since the definition of bravery is not the absence of fear but rather taking action despite it.

11. Seek the Assistance of a Professional:
If you have deeply established self-limiting ideas or they have a substantial influence on your life, you should seriously consider seeing a therapist or counselor for assistance. They can provide direction and assistance in the process of overcoming these ideas.

12. Exercise your capacity for self-awareness:

Maintain a constant vigil on your ideas and feelings. Challenge your self-limiting ideas and work to replace them with more optimistic ways of thinking whenever you become aware that you are doing so.

It is important to keep in mind that eliminating self-limiting ideas is a process that calls for patience as well as persistent effort.

Be nice to yourself, acknowledge your achievements, and realize that shifting these beliefs may lead to a life that is more satisfying and gives you more agency.

You are capable of liberating yourself from the confines of self-limiting ideas and realizing your full potential if you *have the drive and self-awareness to do so.*

Acceptance of Change and Capability to Adapt

Acceptance of change and the capacity to adjust to new circumstances are two abilities that are necessary for navigating the ever-shifting terrain of life, as well as for attaining personal development and success.

The only constant in life is change, and having the ability to adapt enables you to prosper in novel circumstances and triumph over obstacles.

Adaptability and openness to change are essential for the following reasons:

1. Strength and Perseverance in the Face of Adversity:
Being adaptable gives you the capacity to recover quickly from failures and difficulties. You may immediately modify both your thinking and your strategy to identify answers, rather than fighting against the change.

2. Taking Advantage of Opportunities:
Alteration often ushers in brand-new prospects. Embracing change enables you to recognize and make the most of possibilities as they present themselves.

3. Development and Education:
Being adaptable helps to cultivate a growth mindset, which in turn encourages ongoing learning and progress. If you are willing to adapt to changing circumstances, you will be more receptive to gaining new abilities and information.

4. Making the Most of Uncertainty:
Because of this, it is important to be able to adapt to maintain your composure and self-assurance in the face of uncertainty. You get the ability to bravely travel across seas that are unknown to you.

5. Developing Better Decision-Making Capabilities:

Accepting change requires adapting your decision-making process to accommodate shifting conditions. This improves your ability to make decisions, leading to more self-assurance in the paths you've chosen.

6. Boosting Creative Capacity:
Problem-solving ingenuity is often a prerequisite for adaptability. Accepting change and being open to new experiences and perspectives might help you explore creative new avenues and possibilities.

7. Developing Longer-Lasting and Deeper Connections:
Adaptable individuals tend to be more flexible and accommodating, which may lead to improved interactions

with other people. They are eager to get knowledge of a variety of ideas and to find areas of agreement.

8. Taking Advantage of Innovation:
In a world that is always shifting and changing, the capacity to adapt is very necessary for welcoming innovation and propelling it forward. You can keep one step ahead of the competition and be receptive to new ideas if you are willing to adapt to changing circumstances.

9. Developing a Leadership Capability for Resilience:
Effective leaders must be flexible. They need to be confident and have a clear vision as they lead their teams through times of transition and uncertainty.

10. Embracing One's Own Personal Development:

To be adaptable, you often need to force yourself out of your comfort zone. Being open to new experiences and embracing change may both lead to significant personal development.

11. Leaving the Past in the Past:

Being adaptable enables you to let go of things that are no longer beneficial to you. The more you cling to the past, the more difficult it will be to move on, yet accepting change will give you the ability to do so.

12. Acceptance of Difference and Participation:

People that can adapt have a greater willingness to take in new information and experiences. They value the diversity that may be found in people of many origins and cultures.

To accept change and maintain adaptability:

- *Maintain an open mind by always being prepared to consider other theories and points of view.*

- *Always Retain Your Curiosity: Always remember to keep your natural curiosity about the world and your want to learn new things.*

- *Embrace Flexibility: When it comes to your plans and*

strategies, be willing to make adjustments as required.

- *The practice of mindfulness involves being in the here and now while remaining aware of one's thoughts and feelings.*

- *Take some chances, but don't let them consume you, and force yourself to operate outside of your comfort zone regularly.*

- *Acknowledge and rejoice in your capacity for change and development, and enjoy your progress.*

A mentality that enables you to flourish in a changing environment welcomes change and can easily adjust to new circumstances. You may have a more satisfying and successful life by nurturing these abilities, and you can face any problems that come your way with confidence that you can successfully navigate through them.

The Crucial Role of Resilience in Overcoming Obstacles and Failures

The capacity to overcome obstacles with resilience and adaptation is vital in the modern world, with its fast-paced environment.

Whether in our personal or professional lives, every one of us will run against challenges that will test our ability to adapt and prevail. In this issue of the newsletter, we are *going to discuss the significance of being resilient and adaptable, how to cultivate these traits into abilities, and how these traits may be beneficial both in the professional world and in our personal lives.*

In contrast to adaptation, which is the ability to adjust to new circumstances and change, resilience is the capacity to recover after experiencing adversity and adapt to new circumstances. These abilities are essential in the ever-evolving and unpredictable world of today, in which we are constantly confronted with new challenges and situations. Building up our resilience and capacity to adapt allows us to deal with hardship more gracefully and emerge from it in a better position.

The following are some methods that may be used to build the qualities of resilience and adaptability:

-Cultivate a growth mentality A growth mindset is the concept that one's talents can be developed through devotion and hard effort. Cultivating this attitude is believing that one's abilities can be developed. It assists in seeing obstacles, such as setbacks and difficulties, as chances for growth and learning.

-Putting mindfulness into practice is paying attention to the here and now and accepting it without making any kind of value judgments about it. It may assist in lowering stress, strengthening attention, and

enhancing the capacity to regulate emotions, all of which are necessary components of resilience and adaptability.

-Accept the fact that change will occur at some point in the future because those who are more resilient and adaptive are better equipped to deal with it. Making a few tweaks here and there to your routine will help you get more used to living with uncertainty and teach you better-coping mechanisms for it.

-Create a network of support: Having a solid network of support may be beneficial in the process of growing resilience and adaptation. When confronted with obstacles and failures, it might be helpful to surround oneself with individuals who are positive influences and provide support.

-Take care of yourself: the capacity to bounce back from adversity and adjust to new circumstances depends not only on mental toughness but also on one's physical health. It is possible to improve one's general resilience and adaptability by taking care of one's body, which includes maintaining a good diet, receiving an adequate amount of sleep, and engaging in regular physical activity.

It is essential to keep in mind that acquiring the abilities of resiliency and adaptability requires both time and practice. You may develop the abilities you need to manage obstacles *more efficiently if you include these tactics in your day-to-day life and make them a part of your routine.*

Not only are resiliency and flexibility vital in our personal lives, but they are also essential in our professional life. We are required to be resilient and flexible to overcome the obstacles we confront in the fast-paced work world of today. Employers place a high premium on candidates who can easily adjust to new circumstances and quickly recover from failure. Because of these qualities, we can keep our cool under pressure, maintain our concentration, and easily navigate difficult circumstances.

CHAPTER 4

Creating a Winning Attitude

Having a winning attitude is a mentality that enables you to approach life with optimism, drive, and confidence in your capabilities to achieve success. Developing a winning attitude may give you the strength to approach life in these ways. It entails developing constructive patterns of behavior and beliefs that are supportive of your objectives and move you forward on the path to greatness.

Developing a winning mentality may be accomplished via the use of the following main strategies:

1. Monitoring Your Inner Conversation and Replacing Negative

Affirmations with Good Affirmations You should monitor your inner conversation and replace negative affirmations with good ones. Talk to yourself with the same amount of compassion and encouragement as you would give to a close friend.

2. Adopt the perspective That Your talents Can Be grown Through work and Learning Adopt the perspective that your talents can be grown through work and learning. Embrace difficulties as chances for personal development and advancement.

3. Clearly Define Your Goals Define clear goals for yourself that are attainable and in line with your beliefs and long-term ambitions. Break goals down into manageable stages, and don't waver in your dedication to achieving them.

4. Utilize Visualization Methods to Visualize Yourself Attaining Your Objectives and Enjoying Success: By using visualization methods, you may vividly see yourself attaining your objectives and enjoying success. Confidence and motivation may be increased via the use of visualization.

5. Challenges should be seen as stepping stones to achievement rather than as hurdles to be overcome. Embrace them. Take them on with gusto, confident in the knowledge that prevailing over obstacles will result in increased personal development.

6. Put Yourself in a Positive Environment by surrounding yourself with good influences, helpful people, and inspiring information that will boost you up and inspire you.

7. Cultivate an attitude of appreciation by regularly reflecting on all of how your life is blessed. Maintaining an attitude of thankfulness requires regular practice, and it may be applied to both large and little accomplishments.

8. Continue to Be Persistent: In the face of obstacles or defeats, continue to be persistent and resilient. Consider the challenges you face as chances for growth, and keep pushing ahead with steadfast conviction.

9. Celebrate Even the Smallest of Wins: Regardless of how large or tiny an accomplishment may seem, it ought to be celebrated. Your morale will be boosted, and beneficial behaviors will be reinforced, if you acknowledge your progress.

10. Accept Personal Responsibility: Recognise that you are responsible for your actions, decisions, and the results they produce. You give yourself the capacity to make the required adjustments and improvements when you take ownership of your choices.

11. Adopt a solution-oriented attitude, which means that rather than fixating on the problems themselves, you should look for ways to solve them.

When confronted with obstacles, remember to have a proactive attitude.

12. Failures are a necessary part of the learning process; thus, you should welcome them with open arms. Examine what went wrong, draw some lessons from it, and then make use of this newfound information to do better.

13. Contribute to the accomplishments of others by providing support and encouragement in their activities. You may make the atmosphere more pleasant and encouraging for everyone if you focus on elevating the status of others.

14. Maintain Your Dedication to Learning Always look for new ways to develop yourself and your skills, and make learning a priority in your life. Maintain an attitude of openness and curiosity toward gaining new information and abilities.

15. Foster Resilience: Foster resiliency in yourself so that you can recover quickly from challenges and failures. Accept the unpredictability of change while maintaining an open and optimistic attitude.

To cultivate a winning attitude, it is not necessary to be naive or to refuse to acknowledge the existence of difficulties; rather, it is necessary to approach life with optimism, determination, and a conviction in your capacity to accomplish your objectives despite the hurdles you face. You may unleash your full potential and pave the way to success and fulfillment in a variety of facets of your life if you develop a winning mentality and cultivate a winning mindset.

The Crucial Part That Optimism Plays in Accomplishing Goals

The path of life is one filled with unpredictability, taking one to places one has never been before. As is well known, life is full of unexpected occurrences and miraculous occurrences. Because our future is so unpredictable, it is impossible to foresee what will take place right now and in the very next second. This may be exciting, but it can also be nerve-wracking. Whenever something unexpected takes place, it has the effect of throwing our whole universe off kilter. This may leave you feeling terrible inside. One strategy for coping with these unfavorable emotions is to maintain an optimistic outlook. A person may become more robust to the difficulties of life by cultivating the proper sort of attitude, which also paves the way for the individual's growth and general development in all aspects of life.

What exactly is optimism?

An optimistic vision of the future, as well as the capacity to face problems with self-assurance and an amazing amount of faith, are necessary *components of optimism. Being optimistic enables one to recognize and make the most of opportunities. People who have a healthy dose of optimism can see the silver lining in even the darkest of situations. They can maintain a happy attitude regardless of the circumstances, even when things do not go as planned. People who adopt this style of thinking may find that, over time, they experience less stress and have improved mental health. Being optimistic increases the likelihood that you will take charge of the situation rather than allowing it to dominate you. Optimism also increases the likelihood that you will succeed.*

Characteristics of optimistic persons:

- *They expect that the years to come would bring them happiness.*
- *Prepare yourself for the best possible result of the circumstance.*
- *Consider challenges or obstacles to be opportunities for personal development and growth.*
- *Experience an overwhelming sense of appreciation for all the positive aspects of your life.*
- *Even though they acknowledge the flaws, they do not allow them to devour them.*
- *They are not going to let even one bad event color their view of what the future holds for them.*

- *Having a good attitude not just toward oneself but also toward other people.*

Positive outcomes that may result from optimism

1. Enhances the effectiveness as well as the productivity of your work.
Both work happiness and productivity are significantly influenced by one's level of optimism. People who have a positive outlook are often better able to bounce back quickly from setbacks.

They can shrug off failures and continue moving on in life, rather than allowing themselves to get mired in pessimism. The adoption of a constructive mentality enables one to emerge from trying experiences as an even more powerful person and a better version of oneself. They don't wallow in the difficulties; rather, they search for methods to solve the issues and make things better.

It is possible to achieve greater levels of success in one's personal life as well as one's professional life by adopting a more proactive attitude. These individuals share their upbeat and optimistic energy with others around them, which results in a more pleasant working atmosphere and higher levels of morale and productivity within the team.

2. Contributes to the preservation of connections

People who have a positive outlook do not take the things they have for granted but, instead, express their thanks to their partners by showing appreciation for them and by pushing them to accomplish whatever it is they set out to do.

They are a continual source of comfort and support for their loved ones, don't dwell on the possibility of anything going wrong, and have trust in everything. They love their relationships without conditions since they desire the best for both themselves and their spouse at the same time. Because of this viewpoint, people tend to have relationships that are both longer and more rewarding.

When you are willing to engage in new activities and be open to a wide range of experiences, you will have a greater opportunity to connect with others on a meaningful level and make new friends.

3. A positive outlook lowers one's chances of developing anxiety and depression.
People who are optimists look for the positive in every circumstance and face obstacles with full confidence and determination.

This assists in lessening the amount of stress that they are under, which eventually improves their mental health. Pessimists are more inclined than optimists to blame themselves or others for unfavorable occurrences, whilst optimists are less likely to do so.

Instead of focusing on these unsettling emotions, they look for methods to improve their situation in the future so that they can better handle whatever comes their way. No matter how upbeat you are, you cannot completely exclude the possibility that something terrible may occur.

However, if you can train your mind to focus on the good aspects of a situation rather than dwelling on the bad aspects, you will be well on your way to a happier and healthier state of being.

4. Enhancing one's capacity to find solutions to problems

Being receptive to novel concepts and points of view helps a person to search for original solutions by taking into account a variety of possibilities rather than pigeonholing them into a single approach. Because of this, they can investigate and see issues in a highly beneficial way.

5. Strengthens your ability to bounce back from setbacks and challenges
They can pick themselves up and get back on track during the storm more easily than at other times. They believe that they can improve their circumstances if they put in sufficient effort, which keeps them motivated and devoted to achieving their objective.

Optimists are more likely to be resilient in the face of adversity since they don't see things as being permanent or immutable. Optimistic people tend to have better lives overall, including maintaining a healthy weight, engaging in regular physical activity, and going to the doctor for regular exams. As a consequence of this, individuals have a lower risk of suffering from health problems that might lead to challenges.

6. Ability to quickly adjust to different settings and circumstances
The capacity of optimists to adapt is beneficial under challenging circumstances.

They can face adversity, overcome it, and go on with tremendous faith and bravery, which enables them to see the wider picture. When you go to another nation or attempt to adapt to the traditions and norms of a different culture, you will find that optimism is a very helpful tool.

The optimistic view holds that there is always something positive to be found in every given situation.

7. Increases a feeling of mastery and command over one's life
Being optimistic instills a feeling of serenity and tranquility inside you, in addition to a sense of eagerness for what's to come.

Optimistic person tends to be proactive in their approach and generate a significant feeling of control over their own lives. Optimism may make you feel more in control of your life by enhancing your sense of self-confidence and ability. This can lead to a more positive outlook on life. It is much simpler to take action since challenges will not seem to be as insurmountable if you have confidence in yourself and the abilities you possess.

If we are pessimistic and believe that we do not have what it takes to attain our goals, we may be able to persuade ourselves not to take risks or pursue our goals because of this belief. But having a positive outlook on life helps us become more self-assured in our capabilities and gives us the bravery to try new things and work towards the objectives we have established.

Cognitive restructuring is a strategy that helps people become more hopeful.

Cognitive restructuring is a method that involves intentionally confronting negative and self-limiting beliefs to replace them with more positive thinking patterns. This method may help you and others become more optimistic.

The cognitive reorganization process consists of the following five steps:

- Find out what's going on in your life that's causing you to have *negative thoughts and sentiments.*

- *Consider how you feel right now and give it some thought.*
- *Become aware of the negative ideas that are running through your head as a result of the situation.*
- *Examining the data may either confirm or disprove the validity of your pessimistic beliefs.*
- *Maintain your attention only on the objective truth, and work to change any negative, habitual ideas you have into more upbeat, practical ones.*

Keeping One's Attention and Willingness Focused

Willpower and determination are topics that are extensively covered in every success story. A large number of individuals hold the view that these qualities are innate and that successful people just have more of them than others. On the other hand, these individuals will give you a different account and insist that they did not arrive with more drive than others. They will explain to you how they channeled their tenacity and made it work for them to achieve their objectives in a manner that was both efficient and successful.

If you want to achieve the same level of success as they have, you need to learn how to channel your desire effectively.

1. Prepare for the day ahead.

- *You have to make some choices concerning the next day every night before you go to sleep.*
- *You need to make decisions on what you are going to wear, how you are going to get to work, and what you are going to eat for lunch.*
- *It is far simpler to prepare a nutritious lunch the night before, rather than attempting to do so in the morning.*
- *In addition to this, it will prevent you from purchasing your lunch from the hot dog seller located outside the workplace, which is not the best option.*
- *This is also true for situations in which you are required to spend money. You are going to need to*

devise a financial plan that you can adhere to.

- *Before going to bed, give some thought to the following day and make a conscious decision not to check your email until you have completed the activities that were the most important for that day.*
- *In addition to this, you need to keep to the timetable that you make.*
- *You could try closing your eyes at the end of the day and focusing on the satisfying sensation of having been in control throughout the day.*
- *You will find that if you make it a practice to plan out your day, it will be easier for you to make the*

simple choices that tend to slow you down.

- *Because of this, it will be much simpler to steer clear of being sidetracked by thinking about these issues and wasting your time on insignificant particulars.*
- *You will be able to direct your attention to the more significant responsibilities at hand.*

2. *Start with the most challenging tasks.*

- *Your challenging activities will not get any easier if you put them off, and the worry that you feel about them may even make them more difficult to do.*
- *If you put off doing these duties, you will wind up expending mental energy worrying about*

them instead of using that energy to get them done.

- *Because you are alert and have plenty of energy as the day begins, you should focus on completing the tasks that require the most effort first.*
- *Research has shown that our brains are at their most alert in the morning, and to tackle challenging activities, you will need this level of mental acuity.*
- *After you have completed these activities and turned them in, you will be free to focus on the usual work that has been assigned to you.*
- *You will also have the time to handle the less time-consuming and energy-demanding duties*

now that you will have more free time.

3. *Get rid of all the interruptions.*
   - *Real crises will present themselves, and it will be necessary for you to respond appropriately to them.*
   - *On the other hand, the majority of the occurrences that take place will serve just to divert attention; they will not involve genuine crises and will not need an immediate response.*
   - *If you give these problems some time, you'll find that they resolve themselves on their own the vast majority of the time.*
   - *When you react to these types of events, you often put yourself in*

a position to be confronted with more insignificant problems.

- *It is in your best interest to refrain from responding and instead concentrate on the duties at hand.*
- *People will get the impression from this that you are focused on other things and do not have the time to deal with little issues as a result of your actions.*

4. Recharge your batteries and keep your strength up.

- *If you feel that your energy is beginning to wane, you need to stop what you're doing for a moment so that you may regain some of that energy.*
- *You may go for a stroll or engage in another activity that*

diverts your attention from the work and the activity that you are now doing.

- *You will be able to tackle the work more effectively when you return because you will have more concentration than when you left.*

- *Instead of eating a substantial meal during your lunch break, you should focus on eating nutritious meals like fresh vegetables and fruit instead of a heavy dinner.*

- *You also need to make sure that you receive enough exercise and that you consume enough water throughout the day.*

- *You should establish a routine with this in mind so that you do not have to consciously think about them and so that they may become ingrained in your regular activities.*

5. Bring your focus back to the objectives you've set.

- *You need to have a mechanism in place that continually brings to your attention the goal toward which you are working.*
- *It could be helpful to create a mental movie or a vision board. Your reason for pursuing this objective is very important since it will be the driving force behind your success.*
- *If you want to create a school for children from disadvantaged backgrounds and you want to collect a certain amount of money for it, having a distinct*

image of the school can help you concentrate.

- *You should spend five minutes out of each day visualizing achieving your objective, and you should be as specific as possible.*
- *A connection on an emotional level is necessary and will improve your level of motivation.*

You may continue your road toward achievement with a clear head and unwavering drive if you put these tactics into practice. You will certainly face hurdles and diversions; nevertheless, if you keep a resilient mentality and a determined attitude, you will be able to triumph over the challenges you face and accomplish your objectives with distinction.

Adopting a Positive "Can-Do" Attitude

Adopting a "Can-Do" attitude is cultivating an optimistic mentality in which you trust in your capacity to prevail over obstacles and realize your goals despite the presence of adversity. It requires going into challenges and circumstances with self-assurance, resiliency, and a positive, forward-thinking attitude.

The following is a list of ways in which you may develop a "Can-Do" attitude:

1. Believe in Yourself Recognise your strengths and believe that you have the ability, skills, and resolve to achieve the objectives that you have set for yourself.

2. Negative Thoughts Should Be Challenged And Replaced With Positive And Empowering Thoughts To reframe negative thoughts, challenge them and replace them with positive and empowering thoughts. If you find yourself wanting to say "I can't," try asking yourself, "How can I?"

3. When confronted with challenges, rather than fixating on the issue at hand, one should shift their attention to several potential solutions. Always have an attitude focused on finding solutions.

4. Accept Obstacles: Consider obstacles to be opportunities for personal development and advancement. Engage in them with gusto, confident in the knowledge that conquering them will teach you vital lessons in the process.

5. Learn from Your Mistakes Instead of seeing failure as something to be feared, consider it as a necessary step on the path to achievement. You can only grow by reflecting on your past errors and applying what you've learned from them.

6. Put Positive Individuals Around You: Put yourself in an environment where you are surrounded by positive and supporting individuals who believe in your potential. Your

"Can-Do" mentality might be given a boost by their support.

7. Visualization is a powerful tool that may be used to help you see yourself succeeding and attaining your objectives. Imagining oneself achieving achievement boosts self-confidence and drive.

8. Encourage yourself with kind words and acknowledge your accomplishments, no matter how little they may seem. This is an important part of the self-encouragement practice. The mentality of "Can-Do" is boosted when progress is celebrated.

9. Be conscious of the language you use when discussing yourself and your skills, and try to steer clear of

phrases that may be seen as self-limiting. Stay away from terms that put limits on yourself and concentrate on your accomplishments instead.

10. Maintain Your Resilience: To recover quickly from failures and keep your "Can-Do" attitude even when things become difficult, cultivate your resilience.

11. Establish Realistic Goals Establish attainable goals in line with your talents and desires. Your confidence in your ability to achieve your objectives will be bolstered as you make steady headway toward achieving them.

12. Be ready to venture Outside of Your Comfort Zone and Take Calculated Risks You should be ready to venture outside of your comfort zone and take calculated risks. Having a "Can-Do" mindset means being open to chances for personal development and business progress.

13. Focus on work: Regardless of the immediate results of your endeavors, it is important to acknowledge the amount of work you have put into them. Recognize the effort and dedication that you have shown.

14. Honor Your Accomplishments: Honor all of your accomplishments, no matter how large or tiny they may be. A positive mentality is strengthened when accomplishments are acknowledged and celebrated.

15. Maintain Your Dedication: Maintain your dedication to the accomplishment of your objectives and dreams. Maintaining a "Can-Do" mindset requires a steady application of work as well as unwavering commitment.

Adopting a "Can-Do" attitude gives you the ability to tackle difficulties with bravery, follow your ambitions with self-assurance, and have a positive approach to life. You may drive yourself ahead and enable yourself to reach your greatest potential by adopting a mentality that permits you to.

Fostering a "Can-Do" mentality enables one to become more receptive to new experiences and possibilities, both of which are necessary for one's development and advancement toward their goals.

CHAPTER 5

Management of one's time and one's productivity

Time management and productivity are necessary skills that enable individuals to make the most of the time they have available to them, effectively complete their responsibilities, and accomplish their objectives.

The following is a list of methods that can help improve productivity and time management:

1. Determine Your Priorities and Clearly Define Your Goals Prioritize the things that are most important to you. Having well-defined goals provides both direction and concentration.

2. Tasks should be prioritized by determining those that are the most time-sensitive and important and then focusing on completing those tasks first. Utilize methods such as the Eisenhower Matrix to classify tasks according to the importance and level of urgency they require.

3. Make a To-Do List: Create a to-do list either daily or weekly to keep track of the tasks you need to complete and the due dates. This assists you in maintaining organization and makes it more likely that nothing will be overlooked.

4. Apply the technique of time blocking, in which separate chunks of time are set aside for various projects and pursuits. This method is structured, which helps to reduce distractions and improve concentration.

5. *Avoid Multitasking:* Instead of focusing on several different things at once, stick to just one at a time. This makes it easier to concentrate and decreases the likelihood of making mistakes.

6. *Get Rid of Time-Wasters:* Make a list of the activities that take up your time but don't move you closer to achieving your goals, and then get rid of them. Reduce the amount of time you spend on social media, pointless meetings, and activities that aren't necessary.

7. Establish Time Limits: To prevent yourself from devoting an excessive amount of time to any one endeavor, establish time limits for each of your tasks. Make use of timers or alarms to help you keep track of when it is appropriate to move on to the next activity.

8. Learn to Decline: Establish priorities for your commitments and be willing to decline opportunities or requests that do not support your long-term objectives or are outside of your capabilities.

9. When you are faced with large or complicated tasks, you should break them down into smaller steps that are more manageable. They become less intimidating and more manageable as a result of this.

10. Take Frequent Breaks: To prevent burnout and maintain your concentration throughout the workday, it is important to regularly schedule short breaks for yourself. Taking a break from your work can help you become more productive overall.

11. Put an Emphasis on Outcomes, Not Effort Your productivity should be measured not by the amount of time spent on tasks, but rather by the outcomes of those tasks. It is important to prioritize quality over quantity.

12. *Reduce the Number of Distractions* One way to make the working environment more productive is to reduce the number of distractions. To maintain your concentration, you should turn off notifications, close tabs that aren't necessary, and set boundaries.

13. *duties Should Be Delegated:* If at all feasible, duties that other people are capable of doing should be delegated. You can maximize your productivity and concentrate on the activities that are of the highest importance when you delegate.

14. *Reflect and Review:* Make it a habit to regularly reflect on how you manage your time and how productive you are. Determine the

areas in which there is room for improvement and make the required modifications.

15. Invest in Your Personal Development: Learn new things and develop your abilities consistently to increase your productivity and keep one step ahead of difficult situations.

You will be able to maximize the use of the time you have, improve your level of productivity, and achieve more in both your personal and professional lives if you put into practice the following time management and productivity tactics. Keep in mind that increasing your productivity does not imply taking on new responsibilities; rather, it means maximizing the impact of the resources you already have at your disposal.

Learning to Manage Your Time Is the Key to Increased Productivity

Learning to manage your time effectively is very necessary if you want to increase your efficiency and output. Time is a limited resource, and how you choose to use it has a big bearing on both your level of achievement and your quality of life.

The following are some fundamental ideas and methods that, when put into practice, may help you make better use of your time:

1. Establishing Precise Goals and Priorities Define both your long-term and short-term objectives, and then arrange them in ascending order of significance and time constraint. Having a clear understanding of what aspects of your life are most important enables you to better manage your time.

2. Make a Daily Plan: Create a daily plan or a to-do list that defines the activities you need to do to meet your obligations. Plan out your day in a manner that takes into account the things that are most important to you.

3. Utilize the Time-Blocking Method: Allocate distinct time chunks to the various activities and responsibilities that fall within your purview. By using this technique, which is concentrated, distractions are reduced, and attention is improved.

4. Procrastination should be avoided at all costs by first determining why you tend to put things off and then searching for solutions to the problem. Getting a head start on projects might help reduce stress and the need to hurry at the last minute.

5. Give Yourself Specific Time restrictions: Set time restrictions for each of the activities you need to do. According to Parkinson's Law, work will expand to cover the available time; thus, creating deadlines may help enhance productivity.

6. Adhere to the "Two-Minute Rule," which states that if you can do a job in less than two minutes, you should do it right away rather than putting it off.

7. To batch comparable jobs, you should group tasks that are similar together and then perform each one in order. Because of this, the amount of time spent switching between various sorts of activity is reduced.

8. Get Rid of Time-Wasting Activities: Identify activities that don't contribute much to your life or your objectives, and then get rid of them or cut down on how much time you spend on them. This may involve engaging in an excessive amount of activity on social media, attending an excessive number of meetings, or aimlessly perusing the internet.

9. Acquire the Habit of Saying "No" and Exercise Caution When Taking on Additional Commitments. It's okay to turn down requests or chores if they won't help you reach your objectives or would take up too much of your time.

10. assign and Outsource: If it is at all practicable, you should assign some responsibilities to other people or outsource certain activities that other people can manage more effectively. This makes time available for activities with greater priority.

11. Reduce the Number of Distractions One way to make the working

environment more conducive to concentration is to reduce the number of distractions. To maintain your concentration, you should turn off alerts, shut tabs that aren't essential, and set limits.

12. Take Frequent rests: To stay productive throughout the day, it is important to take regular rests that are just a few minutes long. It's possible that taking breaks will make you more productive overall.

13. Review your time management routines regularly and evaluate how successful they are, then make any necessary adjustments. Make any necessary modifications to achieve greater levels of productivity.

14. Invest in Tools That Help You Manage Your Time Make use of productivity apps, calendars, task organizers, or other time-tracking tools to assist you in remaining organized and on track.

15. Continued Improvement: Identify ways in which you may enhance your time management abilities continually and seek the input of others to determine areas in which you can progress.

Having complete control over your time calls for self-discipline, an acute awareness of how you spend your time, and a dedication to making deliberate decisions about how you should spend each minute. You will be able to become more productive, accomplish your objectives, and lead a life that is more balanced and satisfying if you put into practice the following time management ideas and practices.

Keep in mind that time is a very important resource and that if you spend it in a manner that maximizes its potential, it may provide you with enormous benefits in both your personal and professional endeavors.

The Effectiveness of Setting Priorities and Maintaining Focus

The capacity of prioritization and concentration to assist you in making the most of your time, energy, and resources is the source of their respective powers. You may attain *better levels of productivity, efficiency, and success if you first determine what genuinely counts and then focus your efforts on completing the activities that fall under that category.*

The power of prioritization and concentration may be summarized as follows:

1. Increasing Productivity: Setting priorities enables you to concentrate on high-impact activities first, which guarantees that you will make the most of the limited amount of time and resources you have available.

2. The likelihood of your goals being accomplished is improved when you zero in on the activities and objectives that are of the utmost significance to you. You keep from becoming bogged down by tasks that are of lesser significance.

3. Reducing the Feeling of Being Overwhelmed Prioritisation, which involves breaking down large undertakings into smaller, more manageable parts, is one way to reduce the feeling of being overwhelmed. You can maintain your clarity and concentration while doing one activity at a time.

4. Time Management: Establishing priorities enables you to more efficiently divide and use your available time. You focus more on the things that get you closer to achieving your goals and spend less time on activities that are lately necessary.

5. Better Capacity to Decide Prioritization Allows You to Make Educated Choices Doing Prioritisation enables you to make educated choices on where to focus your time, energy, and resources. You give careful consideration to both the significance and the potential outcomes of each option.

6. Reducing stress and mental clutter may be accomplished by concentrating on completing one activity at a time, able to give each action the whole concentration that it requires, which lessens the sensation of being overwhelmed.

7. Improved Work Quality You will be able to produce higher-quality work with fewer mistakes or oversights if you give your undivided attention to the most essential jobs.

8. Increased Productivity: Setting priorities and maintaining concentration can increase productivity by eliminating the need to multitask and encouraging a state of "flow," in which a person is completely absorbed in the activity at hand.

9. When you set priorities and concentrate on what's most important, you'll be in a better position to fulfill deadlines and avoid scrambling at the last minute.

10. Prioritization is a tool that may assist you in striking a healthy balance between the demands of your professional and personal life. You can make time for hobbies outside of work if you prioritize the things that are most important to you.

11. Gaining Momentum and maintaining the desire to continue working productively on additional projects may be achieved by completing high-priority activities first.

12. Capacity for Adaptation: Establishing priorities enables you to respond more effectively to rapidly shifting conditions. You can modify your concentration by changing priorities.

13. *Achieving Clarity: The process of prioritization helps to clarify your goals and removes distractions, which enables you to remain on track and prevents you from spending time on things that are not vital.*

14. *Growing Your Confidence You may grow your confidence in your talents and your ability to make decisions by concentrating on key activities and completing them successfully.*

15. *Establishing a Sense of Purpose may be accomplished via the process of prioritization, which links your day-to-day activities to your long-term objectives and provides you with a sense of direction.*

It takes a lot of self-discipline and practice to become an expert in the art of prioritization and concentration. It requires being deliberate about the activities to which one chooses to commit his or her time and energy.

You may flourish in both your personal and professional endeavors by continuously implementing these concepts, which will unleash the power of prioritization and concentration for you and allow you to do better in both.

The Overcoming of Procrastination and Other Habits That Waste Time

It is crucial to overcome procrastination and behaviors that *waste time if you want to improve your productivity and go closer to accomplishing your objectives. These behaviors may slow down the progress being made, cause undue tension, and cause chances to be lost.*

The following is a list of tactics that may assist you in overcoming procrastination and developing more productive habits:

1. Consider the reasons behind your time-wasting behaviors, such as procrastination or routines that cause you to waste time. It could be anxiety, a lack of drive, an obsession with perfectionism, or a sensation of being overwhelmed. The underlying problems may be addressed more effectively when the fundamental cause has been identified.

2. Tasks should be divided into smaller, more manageable phases so that they may be completed successfully. This makes things less daunting and enables you to make progress more straightforwardly.

3. Establish Clear and Reasonable Deadlines for Each Work It is important to establish clear and reasonable deadlines for each work. Having a time limit not only gives you a feeling of urgency but also makes you more responsible for your actions.

4. Follow the "Two-Minute Rule," which states that if you can do a job in less than two minutes, you should do it right away rather than putting it off.

5. Eliminate Distractions: Determine which distractions result in lost time and strive towards establishing an atmosphere that encourages concentration. Put the alerts on mute, dismiss any tabs that aren't required, and draw some limits.

6. work should be prioritized; your attention should be directed towards high-priority work, and you should avoid becoming sidetracked by less essential activities. To prioritize tasks efficiently, use methods such as the Eisenhower Matrix.

7. Create a schedule: Create a schedule for yourself on a daily or weekly basis that involves setting aside time for the chores that are most essential to you. Having a well-structured routine may help reduce the amount of time spent putting things off.

8. Establish prizes and punishments: Establish a system of prizes for completing work on time, as well as a set of punishments for those who are unable to fulfill their deadlines. This provides additional incentive to continue on the correct path.

9. Utilize the Pomodoro Technique, which entails working for concentrated periods, often 25 minutes, followed by a brief rest. This helps keep one's focus up and prevents mental exhaustion.

10. Accepting your imperfections is important since striving for perfection might cause procrastination. Recognize that not everything has to be flawless to make progress, and instead concentrate on making progress.

11. Imagine the pleasant results that will come from finishing your duties on schedule and reaching your objectives, and keep those images in your mind while you work. The power of visualization may help boost motivation.

12. Seek Accountability: Discuss your objectives and achievements with a

third party who is in a position to keep you responsible. The presence of a support system might help you stay motivated and on track to achieve your goals.

13. Be kind to yourself and refrain from being too hard on yourself if you ever find yourself in a difficult situation. Be sympathetic, and direct your attention towards gaining knowledge from your experiences to better go ahead.

14. Whenever it's feasible, put a limit on the number of options available. This will help you avoid decision fatigue. Simplify your routine and get rid of any decisions that aren't required.

15. You may set yourself up for success by beginning each day with a job that is manageable and relatively straightforward. This will give you a feeling of achievement, which will motivate you to go on.

Both overcoming procrastination and breaking behaviors that waste time take regular work and an awareness of one's tendencies. You may improve your effectiveness, lower your stress levels, and make substantial headway toward achieving your objectives if you apply the ideas outlined here and cultivate more productive habits.

Keep in mind that this is a step-by-step approach and that recognizing each progress along the way will help perpetuate the beneficial improvements.

CHAPTER 6

Surrounding Yourself with Success

As we progress and develop in both our personal and professional lives, we must surround ourselves with people who encourage and inspire us to be our best selves. The people with whom we surround ourselves have a major impact on how we think, the things we believe, and the things we do. Because of this, we must surround ourselves with people who are achieving more success than we are.

People who are doing better than us are people who have achieved more in their life and have more experience in the sectors in which they work than we do. We can obtain insights and information that would have taken us *years to acquire on our own if we had not surrounded ourselves with people who have the experiences, perspectives, and perspectives that they have.*

For example, if you want to be an entrepreneur someday, it would be very useful for you to surround yourself with other great entrepreneurs who have established successful firms from the ground up. These business owners have a wealth of experience and knowledge to share on the proper and improper ways to launch a new company. They may also share their own experiences with you and guide you to assist you avoid making prevalent errors.

Additionally, associating oneself with others who are more successful than you might also serve as a source of motivation for you. Observing other people who have succeeded in achieving remarkable goals might serve as inspiration for you to pursue remarkable achievements in your own life. It has the potential to instill in you the motivation and resolve to push yourself toward achieving your objectives and dreams.

As a human, it is beneficial to surround yourself with people who are farther along in life than you are. Not only will this help you learn and be inspired, but it will also help you grow and develop as a person. These people can push you to think creatively and view the world from a variety of angles, which may be beneficial to you. They may also assist you in honing your talents and refining the way you approach finding solutions to issues.

In addition, it is helpful to construct a support system by surrounding oneself with individuals who are farther along in their path than you are. When you are in the most desperate need of encouragement and support, these people can provide it to you. As you work towards achieving your objectives, they may also help hold you responsible and ensure that you stay on track.

It is vital to remember why you want to be in this kind of atmosphere in the first place. Surrounding yourself with *people who are performing better than you may be very useful; however, it is also necessary to remember why you want to be in this sort of environment in the first place. Is it because you want to improve as a person via interaction with them, gain knowledge from them, or just be driven by them? No of the cause, you should ensure that you are aware of the motivation for surrounding yourself with the people you are.*

It is of the utmost significance to surround oneself with successful individuals because...

1.   They can act as examples for others to follow. When you witness someone successful in their work or their personal life, it may be motivating and give you a feeling of what is possible for you to do as well.

This may provide you with a road map for what you need to do to go to where you want to be if you are in a similar field or have similar objectives; it can be quite effective if you are in a similar profession or have similar ambitions.

You may learn from the experiences of those who have already achieved success, ask them for guidance, and receive vital insights into what it takes to be successful if you surround yourself with successful people.

2. They can assist you in networking. The company you keep may open doors for you, put you in

touch with individuals who can be of assistance to you in your professional or personal life, and even give you crucial connections.

When you surround yourself with successful people, you boost your chances of being exposed to new possibilities and developing key connections that may help you accomplish your objectives. If you want to be successful, surround yourself with successful people.

3. They have an optimistic attitude and see themselves as capable of continuous improvement. They are constantly on the lookout for ways in which they might better themselves and their circumstances, and they are not hesitant to take chances or experiment with new things.

You will be able to acquire a similar mentality and grow more confident in your talents if you surround yourself with the sorts of individuals described above. You may also learn how to be more resilient and how to bounce back from failures, which are both crucial skills for success in whatever career you choose to pursue.

In addition to all of these advantages, surrounding yourself with successful individuals may assist you in maintaining your motivation and keeping your attention on your objectives. It's easy to feel disappointed about one's development and accomplishments when one observes others making headway and enjoying success.

However, if you associate yourself with others who are farther along in their endeavors than you are, it might help you remain motivated and focused on the objectives you have set for yourself. You can see for yourself what is attainable and what steps need to be taken to achieve your goals.

The question now is how you can ensure that you are surrounded by successful individuals.

The first thing you need to do is think about the kinds of individuals you wish to have in your life. These might be individuals you are close to, people you look up to from a distance or even people you haven't even had the chance to meet yet.

After you have selected the people you want to surround yourself with, the next step is to begin cultivating connections with those individuals. This might involve getting in touch with them and asking for guidance, joining or attending events where they will be present, or even just following them on social media and interacting with them there.

Joining organizations or groups whose aims and pursuits are congruent with your own is yet another strategy you may use to surround yourself with successful individuals. This may include mastermind groups, networking groups, professional organizations, or even internet communities. By participating in these kinds of organizations, you will have the opportunity to network with individuals who are more successful than you and who have interests and objectives that are comparable to your own.

Last but not least, it is essential to keep in mind that surrounding yourself with people who are more successful than you is not about measuring your success against that of others but rather about gaining knowledge from those around you and maturing as a person.

Consequently, you must think about why you want to be in this setting and what you intend to achieve as a result of being here. After that, initiate contact with people who inspire you and work to cultivate a connection with them.

___The Influence That Your Social Circle Has on Your Achievements___

Your network of friends and acquaintances has a considerable bearing on both your professional accomplishments and your general quality of life. Your circle of friends and acquaintances has the potential to shape not just your frame of mind but also your routines, opportunities, and, eventually, your path to realizing your ambitions.

The following are some of how the people in your social circle might influence your level of success:

1. Attitude & Mindset: The mindsets and attitudes of the people in your social circle have the potential to infect you. Being in the company of optimistic and ambitious people may motivate you to adopt a similar mentality, which in turn can lead to improved self-assurance and the desire to work towards achieving your objectives.

2. Encouragement, validity, and Emotional Support Having a supportive social circle can give encouragement, validity, and emotional support when times are

tough. This assistance has the potential to strengthen your resilience and assist you in remaining dedicated to pursuing your goals.

3. Accountability means that other people will be able to hold you responsible for your activities if you communicate your objectives and your progress with them. This responsibility might help you stay on track and keep your attention on the goals you have set for yourself.

4. Opportunities and Connections: The people in your social circle may be able to introduce you to advantageous opportunities and connections for networking. Establishing connections with influential people may lead to the discovery of new possibilities and the formation of new partnerships.

5. Interacting with smart and successful people may broaden your exposure to fresh experiences, ideas, and viewpoints, all of which are important for personal development. Your personal and professional development may be accelerated by gaining knowledge from the perspectives of others.

6. motivation and Role Models: Being in the company of successful people may serve as a source of motivation for those who are in their company. Motivating yourself to attain success for yourself may be as simple as looking at the accomplishments of others and thinking about how they overcame obstacles.

7. Pessimism and Limiting Views A social circle that is unsupportive or negative may foster limiting views and pessimism. Likewise, limiting beliefs might prevent one from achieving their full potential. It might slow you down and make you feel less confident in your ability to do what you set out to do.

8. Taking Risks and Being Innovative: If you surround yourself with people who support and encourage you to take risks and be innovative, it will be easier for you to break out of your comfort zone and pursue new chances.

9. Work-Life Balance: The people in your social circle have the potential to impact how you approach striking a work-life balance. Being in the company of people who place a priority on their health and wellness might motivate you to strike a good balance in your own life.

10. Emotional Well-Being A good influence on your emotional well-being may be had via the presence of supportive connections and social interactions that are favorable. This emotional support has the potential to boost both your general happiness and your resistance to stress.

11. Collaboration and Teamwork: Surrounding yourself with people who place a high value on collaboration and teamwork will help to build a climate that is conducive to cooperation, allowing you and your associates to accomplish more as a group.

12. Self-Reflection and Feedback: The people in your social circle may supply you with insightful feedback and comments that can help you become more self-aware and work on improving yourself.

13. Defying Norms and Stereotypes Being a member of a varied social circle may help you break stereotypes and see things from new points of view, which can lead to increased creativity and the ability to solve problems in novel ways.

14. *Personal and Professional Development A social circle that is focused on growth may serve as a source of motivation for you to make consistent investments in both your personal and professional development.*

15. *The act of celebrating one's victories helps to create a good atmosphere that encourages further effort and achievement when it is shared with one's social group.*

It is of the utmost importance to choose the individuals with whom you surround yourself with care and deliberation. The development of a social network that encourages and inspires you along your path to success may have a significant bearing on the trajectory of that trip.

You may cultivate a setting that encourages you to flourish and accomplish any goals you set for yourself if you have an open mind and look for meaningful relationships and good influences. Keep in mind that achieving success is not simply the province of the individual; rather, it is often the product of group effort and cooperation.

Seeking Advice and Assistance from Elders

It is important and beneficial to seek out mentoring and advice as a proactive move toward one's personal and professional development. The act of creating a connection with *someone who has greater experience, knowledge, and wisdom in a certain subject or facet of life is what constitutes the practice of mentorship. This mentor will give you assistance, advice, and direction to assist you in overcoming problems, developing skills, and accomplishing your objectives.*

The following are some of the reasons why seeking out a mentor is so crucial, as well as some tips on how to do so:

1. Acquiring Valuable Insights A mentor may provide invaluable advice and information by drawing on their own life experiences to share with their mentee. They may present you with insights and viewpoints that you may not have previously considered.

2. Personal and Professional Growth: Having a mentor may speed up both your personal and professional growth by assisting you in acquiring skills and information that are pertinent to your goals.

3. Avoiding Common Errors and Obstacles: Having a mentor may assist you in avoiding common errors and obstacles that you may have come across on your path.

4. Opportunities to Expand Your Network A mentor may put you in touch with influential people in your industry, increasing the size of your network and the range of opportunities available to you.

5. Increasing One's Confidence Having a mentor who has faith in one's capabilities and potential may be a great boost to one's confidence and belief in one's potential.

6. Accountability: A mentor can help keep you responsible for your objectives and commitments, which will assist you in maintaining your momentum and maintaining your concentration.

7. Encouragement and Support: When you are going through difficult circumstances, having a mentor may give you encouragement and support, which can help you remain resilient and motivated.

8. Learning through Experience: The experience of a mentor may provide you with a plethora of information to learn from, which can save you time and effort as you go through the process of learning.

9. Advice suited to Your Specialized Circumstances and Goals A mentor may provide you with specialized advice and direction that is suited to your unique circumstances and goals.

10. Broadening Your Horizons: Having a mentor may broaden your horizons by introducing you to new concepts, possibilities, and points of

view that you would not have come across on your own.

11. *Growth Through Challenging Experiences:* A good mentor will encourage you to go beyond your comfort zone and take on new challenges so that you may develop personally.

12. *Functioning as a Good Role Model:* A mentor may function as a good role model for you, motivating you to strive for higher heights.

13. *Developing a Support System:* Mentors often become a part of a person's support system, and they assist in all phases of a person's life and career.

14. Long-Term Relationships: The act of mentoring may pave the way for enduring friendships that are founded on trust and appreciation for one another.

15. Paying It Forward: As you progress and improve as a result of having a mentor, you could eventually have the chance to become a mentor yourself and have a good influence on the lives of other people.

Take into consideration the procedures below to choose a mentor:

- *Find a mentor who is an expert in the areas or talents you want to grow by first determining what particular areas or skills you want to develop and then looking for a mentor who specializes in those areas.*

- *Request suggestions: Speak with coworkers, friends, and other members of your professional network to request suggestions for possible mentors.*

- *Make Contact: After you've located a possible mentor, make contact with them and let them know that you're interested in receiving mentoring from them.*

- *Remember that your mentors are likely very busy people, therefore it is important to show them respect for their time. Show consideration for both their time and their agenda.*

- *Set Clear Expectations: Before beginning the mentoring connection, it is important to establish clear expectations regarding the nature of the relationship, including the frequency of meetings and the outcomes you want to accomplish.*

- *Be Thankful: Never forget to show your thanks and appreciation to your mentor for all of the help and direction they have given you.*

Keep in mind that mentoring is a relationship that goes in both directions. Maintain an attitude that is receptive to new information, be proactive in your search for direction, and show that you are eager to put what you have learned into practice. You can invest in both your personal and professional progress and put yourself on the road to greater success and satisfaction by actively seeking mentoring and advice.

Establishing Mutually Beneficial Relationships and Networks

It is essential to both one's personal and professional development to cultivate connections and networks of support. A solid support network may be an invaluable source of encouragement, direction, and opportunity, assisting you in overcoming obstacles and realizing your ambitions.

Developing helpful connections and networks may be accomplished via the following steps:

1. Determine Your Objectives You should be clear on both your personal and professional objectives to determine the kind of assistance you need. Different aims may call for various kinds of partnerships and networks.

2. Maintain a Friendly and Authentic Attitude When Communicating with Others: Maintain a pleasant, accessible, and genuine attitude. Creating authentic connections is the first step in building helpful partnerships.

3. Take a Genuine Interest in Other People's Interests, Passions, and objectives Take a genuine interest in the interests, passions, and objectives of other people. Building genuine relationships with other people requires you to have strong listening and empathic skills.

4. Participating in Communities Joining communities, clubs, or organizations that are relevant to your hobbies or field of work may be beneficial. These organizations provide the chance to interact with others who have similar values and interests.

5. Participate in Networking Events: Increasing the number of people in your network may be accomplished by participating in networking events, conferences, and seminars. Maintain an attitude that is receptive to starting discussions and introducing oneself to new people.

6. Utilize Social Media: Make use of the many social media platforms available to network with other industry experts and people. To increase your online profile, participate in relevant conversations and contribute stuff that others will find useful.

7. Find a Mentor and a Mentee: When searching for a mentor and a mentee, look for someone who can guide you and someone who can benefit from your expertise and experience. Relationships based on mentoring

may be beneficial for both parties involved.

8. Be Willing to provide Assistance and Support: Be prepared to provide assistance and support to other people without anticipating receiving anything in return. Generosity and supportiveness are two qualities that promote good partnerships.

9. Work Together on Projects: Look for chances to work together with other people on various projects or initiatives. Working together towards a common goal may result in deeper connections as well as more success for everyone involved.

10. Participate in Online Forums and Groups: Join online forums and groups that are relevant to your field or the topics that interest you the most. Participate in conversations, educate others, and network with other people who are interested in the same things you are.

11. Attending Industry Events Going to events and conferences that are particular to your industry is a great way to network with other professionals working in your area. These events are perfect for making new contacts and keeping abreast of the latest developments in the business.

12. After getting to know new individuals, it is important to follow up with them and keep up a consistent line of contact to cultivate new connections.

13. Demonstrate thanks It is important to demonstrate thanks to people who have encouraged you or assisted you on your path. A straightforward expression of gratitude goes a very long way toward preserving strong connections.

14. Maintain a Reputation That Is Dependable and Trustworthy: You may earn the confidence of people by maintaining a reputation that is dependable and trustworthy. Building helpful partnerships requires establishing and maintaining trust.

15. Be Open to Diversity: It is important to be open to diversity and to cultivate connections with people who come from a variety of experiences and backgrounds. The various insights and possibilities that may be gained via diverse networks.

The investment of time and energy required to cultivate supportive connections and networks is more than justified by the many rewards that result. Your life may be enriched, you can get useful insights, and it can help the success of both your personal and professional endeavors if you surround yourself with folks who are supportive and optimistic. Keep in mind that helpful relationships are a two-way street and that investing in these connections can deepen the bonds and establish a support structure that is beneficial to all parties involved.

CHAPTER 7

Accepting Defeat and Gaining Wisdom from Missteps

A key attitude that may lead to personal development, resiliency, and eventually success is willingness to embrace failure and learn from it when it occurs. While it's true that failure may be upsetting, it also presents invaluable chances for learning and growing as a person.

The following is a guide on how to accept defeat and make the most of obstacles:

1. Make a mental shift and start seeing setbacks as opportunities for growth rather than as definitive conclusions. Consider this a chance to broaden your horizons and improve your skills.

2. Recognise that you are not flawless and come to terms with the fact that everyone makes errors and runs across roadblocks. Accept the fact that the process of learning is inherently faulty.

3. Take some time to analyze what went wrong and to reflect on the variables that led to the failure so that you can avoid making the same mistakes again. Finding out what's at the bottom of a problem may help you solve it more effectively in the future.

4. Lessons to Be Learned: Despite the setback, there are still important lessons to be learned. Think about

10. Celebrate Your Efforts: Regardless of the result, you should celebrate your efforts and the progress you've made. Recognize that each step in the right direction is a successful accomplishment.

11. Failure is an inevitable step on the path to achievement, so you shouldn't be afraid of it. Instead, cultivate a positive attitude towards it, understanding that it's only a part of the process.

12. Put Yourself in a Supportive Environment Put yourself in an environment where you are surrounded by people who can provide you empathy and encouragement when things are difficult.

13. Imagine yourself Succeeding Imagine yourself prevailing over challenges and achieving success despite failures. A resilient attitude may be strengthened via the use of positive visualization.

14. Never stop moving forward; do not allow setbacks to immobilize you. Keep moving ahead, even if it's just by a few inches at a time. It's possible to make great headway with consistent work.

15. Studying the lives and experiences of others who have already achieved success may teach you valuable lessons. A significant number of successful people have experienced setbacks on their journey toward reaching their objectives.

Keep in mind that the obstacles and setbacks you face are not an indication of your value or ability. These situations provide chances for personal development and advancement. You may become more resilient, flexible, and better prepared to fulfill your objectives by learning from setbacks and embracing failure as an essential component of the path to success. Failure should be seen as an intrinsic part of the process of achieving success.

Acquiring an Understanding of the Value of Defeat

People have a strong desire to succeed in all they do. Many individuals have a strong aversion to losing, and they express this aversion in a variety of contexts, including games, sports, and other activities. They have the desire to be the center of attention and take the stage in front of other people. While many individuals place a high value on being competitive, others believe that learning from one's errors and failings is of more significance. There is nothing to be embarrassed of when it comes to failure. Failure is an inevitable part of everyone's life, and even though it may be painful, it also has numerous advantages, some of which include being more humble, expanding one's knowledge, and improving one's spiritual strength.

To begin, the only way to grow as a person is via experiencing both success and failure. Everyone is interested in learning how to execute tasks in the most effective manner possible. They have a strong desire to succeed and complete all of their tasks without making any mistakes. Even if there are a lot of individuals who desire to accomplish this goal, there is no way to do it without risking failure. You may learn how to manage your errors for the next time you might confront them from the lessons that failure can offer you. It may show you the steps you need to take to accomplish what you set out to do. You can only really learn what is wrong and what is good via experiencing failure. As you can see, this is one of the advantages that comes from experiencing failure.

In addition, it teaches you to have humility when you succeed. People are quick to celebrate their successes, but many of them do so in a manner that is disruptive to others around them and without considering the environment. However, when they are unsuccessful, they develop a bad attitude and get irritable over their errors. Failure may help you become more modest, even though being humble is difficult. Failure teaches you to recognize when you are right and when you are wrong, and it also teaches you how to properly appreciate your successes. For instance, if I accomplished anything, I used to feel arrogant about it. Because of the numerous times that I have failed, however, I have learned how to regulate my emotions and I have also learned how to be humble.

Failure not only makes you physically stronger, but it also makes you spiritually stronger. Everyone agrees that one's physical capabilities are far more essential than one's spiritual capabilities. Even while this could be true for certain individuals, having a strong spirit is much more essential than having a strong body, and the only way to discover this is via failure. The ability to fail at anything allows you to dedicate more time and energy to achieving your objectives and gives you the confidence to do so. The experience of falling short of your goals might fortify your resolve and make it more difficult for you to quit. I have been unsuccessful several times, and as a result, I have worked even more diligently to attain my objectives. One of the most important advantages of experiencing failure is the opportunity to develop one's spirituality.

Falling short of our goals, despite the challenges that they might provide, is an inevitable aspect of life that ultimately helps us become better individuals. There are so many upsides to failing that you probably weren't aware of any of them at all. For instance, when you try something and it doesn't work out, you learn something new, it teaches you humility, and it helps you become spiritually stronger. You will become a better person overall, and in the future, you will have success just like any other person would if you had an understanding of what failing can do to a person. Therefore, the next time you experience failure, think of it as a positive experience.

Several advantages can only be gained via experiencing failure; these advantages cannot be gained in any other manner. Failure is a necessary step on the path to success; it's just that we don't typically hear about that aspect of a successful person's narrative. The fact that we, as well as our students, will inevitably experience failure does not mean that the game is over.

Therefore, adopt a constructive mentality towards setbacks, and you will discover that they may serve as the impetus for:

1. Clarity
It will bring you down to earth faster than anything else! Failure will raise questions about if everything is really as it appears and whether there is anything else happening that needs to be investigated. In addition to this, it enables us to understand things more plainly and precisely, and it teaches us the important distinction between a sound concept and a flawed one. The most essential question in life is answered by failure: what did I do wrong, and how can I become better? Because of this, the world is a better place, the atmosphere in our

classrooms is happier, and both we and our students are one step closer to achieving our goals.

2. Growth
The learning that may come from making mistakes is enormous. When we recognize that our shortcomings are in our work rather than in ourselves, it is far simpler to pick ourselves up and try again. When we have attempted something and been unsuccessful, we are forced to adapt and adjust our approach. This stimulates the flow of new ideas, which is important since many groundbreaking discoveries and advancements have sprung from utter defeat. We develop more resiliency, strength, and maturity as time goes on.

3. Freedom

When we no longer have to worry about failing because we have already done so, we can enter a new realm of boldness and production. We are aware that falling short of our goals is not the end of the world but rather the building block for something else and more successful. It releases us from the burden of believing or maintaining the impression that we are flawless and have everything under control. Everyone makes errors, so why not accept responsibility for them, acknowledge them, and learn from them? This is a foolproof method that can soften the blow of our blunders and save us from hiding in a corner with a box of tissues when we screw up, so give it a try!

You shouldn't allow failure to get you down; rather, you should utilize it as a stepping stone to something more fantastic.

The following is a list of seven astonishing advantages of failing, which will transform your fear of failing into a source of empowerment.

1. You find that you are organically becoming stronger on the inside.

The capacity for mental toughness and fearlessness, along with the ability to persevere and build resilience despite the magnitude of one's setbacks, is the single trait that distinguishes those who are successful from those who are not.

To turn adversity into an opportunity requires mental toughness, which can be developed through repeated experiences of setbacks.

Coming back from a setback makes you mentally stronger, which in turn makes you more resilient to additional setbacks.

The more times you fail at something, the more likely it is that you will have the capacity to recover fast and think critically to come up with fresh ideas that will make your subsequent effort successful.

You'll develop the mental fortitude, resolve, and motivation necessary to avoid experiencing failure in the future.

2. It completely changes how you look at things.
People who can pick themselves up and try again after experiencing setbacks have a broader perspective and a deeper comprehension of the reasons why they failed.

More complete and insightful knowledge will shift where the responsibility for that failure should be placed.

They are more inclined to attribute their failure to anything that they did improperly or the process itself, both of which are mutable and may be improved upon for the subsequent effort.

People who are severely impacted by failure often blame their attributes, such as not being bright enough, or feel as if they do not deserve success. They are under the impression that they are responsible for the situation, rather than the external factors or the real timing and procedures.

3. You start to grasp the full extent of your potential.
You can't realize your entire potential, beat your personal best, or accomplish the impossible if you're afraid of failing along the way. Your anxiety will simply prevent you from contributing all you have to the cause.

Failure will help you overcome your fear, allowing you to get closer to achieving your goals and aspirations.

If you want to accomplish something, whether it's a goal, a dream, or a desire, you have to be willing to accept the inevitable setbacks you'll have along the road, even if they don't amount to total failure.

The first step towards future success and being the greatest version of yourself is to acknowledge and be okay with the possibility of failing at anything.

4. It bolsters the resolve and resolve of character.

The best way to strengthen your character is to put yourself in situations where you are likely to fail.

Your fortitude, dedication, bravery, and commitment will be put to the test when you have to deal with initiatives that did not go as planned or altogether failed. However, if you can pick yourself up and start again, you may demonstrate to yourself that you have the strength of character to overcome adversity.

5. You automatically acquire the skills of working harder and smarter.
Many individuals who have achieved significant success have said that their greatest setbacks ultimately served as their greatest sources of inspiration.

They are motivated to do better the following time because of this factor.

They devise a plan to protect themselves from repeating the mistake that was made.

6. You are aware of both your capabilities and your limitations.
If you are entirely open to learning as much as you can from your mistakes, you will be able to recognize any deficiencies or shortcomings that you may have.

Once they have been recognized, you will be able to work on improving them or perhaps find someone to collaborate with who can take over those weaknesses so that you may focus on your strengths.

7. You seek inspiration from a variety of different places.

Your inability to achieve success compels you to reevaluate your strategy, think critically, and come up with innovative solutions by "thinking outside the box." As you look for a solution to a problem, you will often find that talking with other people sparks your creative thinking.

It's natural to be afraid of falling short of your goals.

The vast majority of individuals have a tough time admitting that they are not "good enough."

Nevertheless, how one responds to defeat is a question of perspective.

Those who have achieved the most success are aware of the fact that failure is but one of the many stepping stones that lead to achievement. Never allow the possibility of failing to prevent you from going for your goals.

Change your attitude and learn from your mistakes for the next time you experience failure.

The Growth Mindset: Being Willing to Learn from Your Errors

It is the conviction that one's skills and intellect can be improved via the application of undivided attention, persistent effort, and readiness to gain knowledge from one's errors. Individuals who embrace a growth mindset are more likely to see failures and other types of setbacks as chances for development and progress rather than as constraints that are fixed in place.

The following are some of the ways that having a growth mindset is crucial to learning from mistakes:

1. Accepting Challenges People who have a growth mindset look at difficulties as exciting chances to learn new things and improve their existing abilities. They are not scared to tackle challenging responsibilities, even if there is a possibility that they may make errors along the road.

2. Failure is Seen as a Source of Feedback and Not as an Indication of

Incompetence People who have a growth mindset regard failure not as an indication of incompetence but as a source of important feedback. They do a debriefing with themselves, identify the key takeaways, and implement the recommendations.

3. Perseverance and Effort: People who have a growth mindset recognize that becoming an expert in any field needs a lot of hard work and attention to the subject matter. They are prepared to put in a lot of effort because they are aware that the only way to become better is to practice a lot and learn from their mistakes.

4. Putting an Emphasis on Learning: A growth mindset places more of an emphasis on learning itself, as opposed to putting all of one's attention entirely on accomplishing a certain goal. It is believed that the process of continuous development is more vital than quick accomplishment.

5. Putting Self-Limiting Beliefs and Assumptions to the Test The growth mindset puts self-limiting beliefs and assumptions to the test. People that have a growth mindset don't consider their capabilities to be static; rather, they look for ways to improve their intellectual capacity and practical competence.

6. Creating a Culture of Continuous Improvement by Learning from Errors One of the best ways to create a culture of continuous improvement is to learn from your errors. People that have a growth mindset are always motivated to learn new things and get fresh insights to improve their comprehension and overall performance.

7. Redefining "Failure" The term "failure" is redefined in a growth mindset as "not yet." If a person hasn't attained their intended goal, it simply indicates that they haven't accomplished it yet but may still improve with effort and learning.

8. Developing Resilience: Making and learning from errors is one of the best ways to develop resilience, which enables people to recover quickly from defeats and maintain their

motivation in the face of difficult circumstances.

9. Taking Reasonable Risks: Individuals who have a growth mindset are encouraged to take reasonable risks, with the knowledge that they will learn and develop as a result of the experience, even if they run into problems along the way.

10. Feedback is something that people who have a growth mindset deliberately seek to broaden their understanding of their performance and obtain new ideas on how they may improve.

11. In a growth mindset, one celebrates their effort and development regardless of whether or not the end objective has been accomplished. This is because they believe that the journey itself is the reward. Recognizing the path traveled and the progress made is the primary emphasis of this activity.

12. Becoming Out of the "Fixed Mindset" Trap People who have a growth mindset can keep themselves from becoming caught in the "fixed mindset" trap, in which they feel that their talents cannot be improved upon. Instead, they make it a point to foster a growth-oriented mindset via their daily activities.

13. Fostering Curiosity Curiosity and a quest for knowledge may both be fostered by adopting a growth mindset. It inspires people to open

themselves up to new experiences and take on new tasks.

14. Motivating and Inspiring Others: Individuals may inspire and encourage others to embrace continual learning and progress by modeling a growth mindset for others to observe and emulate.

15. An authentic desire for learning and personal progress may be cultivated by adopting a growth mindset, which views failures and difficulties as chances to learn and expand one's capabilities rather than as obstacles to overcome.

Individuals are encouraged to approach life with an open mind and a readiness to learn from their errors while adopting a growth mentality, which is part of the overall growth mindset. It gives people the ability to accept obstacles, develop resilience, and continually progress, which eventually leads to higher levels of success in both their personal and professional lives.

Applying Lessons Learned from Defeat to Future Attempts at Success

The only way to achieve success is via experiencing failure first. Those who can recover from a setback can realize their full potential as a result. The spirit of competition focuses on the common ideals of people who are going through difficult experiences. People who have reached the pinnacle of their field often have compelling life narratives that emphasize the importance of persistence, honesty, and hard work.

The most effective and game-changing method for dealing with obstacles is to see failure as a stepping stone on the path to achievement. Setbacks may be transformed into chances for personal development and advancement if the individual adopts the mindset that failure is an essential step on the path to accomplishment as well as an instructive educational experience.

Here's how to turn your past mistakes into building blocks for future success:

1. Adopt the Belief That Abilities and Intelligence Can Be Developed Through Effort and Study Adopt the belief that abilities and intelligence can be developed through effort and study. Consider each setback an opportunity to grow as a person rather than a critique of the skills you already possess.

2. Take the time to investigate the factors that led to the defeat and learn from your mistakes. Determine what went wrong, what you might have done better, and what important lessons you can take away from the event.

3. Reframe Failure: Failure should be reframed as a normal and unavoidable part of the process of achieving success. It is not a dead end but rather a stepping stone toward ultimate achievement and further advancement.

4. Pay Attention to Your Efforts and Accomplishments: Regardless of the Outcome, You Should Celebrate Your Efforts and Accomplishments. Be conscious of the fact that each success takes you that much closer to achieving your objectives.

5. Consider Every Defeat an Opportunity to Learn: When something doesn't go as planned, look at it as an opportunity to rethink your strategy and test out some new ideas. It is an opportunity to change course, make adjustments, and hone your strategy for achieving success.

6. Embrace defeat as a method of developing your resilience; this will help you become more resilient. Your resilience and capacity to endure in the face of adversity will increase to the degree that you are successful in overcoming difficulties and defeats.

7. Stay Away From Negative Self-Talk And Self-Blame Stay away from negative self-talk and self-blame. Exercise compassion for yourself and recognize that everyone has setbacks along the path they choose to travel.

8. Maintain a Positive Mindset It is important to remember to have a positive mindset and to concentrate on finding solutions to problems rather than concentrating on the failures themselves. A more optimistic outlook improves one's ability to find solutions to problems.

9. Make an effort to get help and Feedback Make an effort to get help from mentors, coworkers, or friends. They may provide you with insights and criticism that will assist you in learning from the event and growing as a result of it.

10. Make required Adjustments: To succeed in the future, you must first understand how to adapt your approach and then make the required adjustments. Maintain an open mind toward new ideas and changes.

11. Establish Realistic Expectations: Ensure that you have reasonable expectations for yourself and recognize that achieving success often includes overcoming obstacles along the way.

12. Maintain Your Determination: Despite experiencing setbacks, you should not waver in your determination to achieve the objectives you have set for yourself. To transform failure into success, one of the most important factors is perseverance.

13. Maintain Your Curiosity It is important to maintain your curiosity and be open to trying new things. Curiosity enables one to investigate previously unconsidered options and play with a greater degree of uncertainty.

14. Imagine Yourself prospering Despite the Obstacles You Face Take this setback as a chance to imagine yourself prospering despite the challenges you face. The power of positive visualization may help you feel more confident in your ability to achieve your objectives.

15. Continue to Move Forward: Do not let past failures deter you from pursuing your goals and achieving your aspirations. Continue moving ahead, gaining knowledge from each new experience, and seeing setbacks as opportunities to learn and grow in preparation for ultimate success.

Keep in mind that many successful people have experienced a significant number of setbacks on their journey toward reaching their objectives. You may embrace development, learning, and resilience by seeing failure as a stepping stone to success. In doing so, you will put yourself on the road to attaining the goals that you have set for yourself. Every failure is a chance to learn something new, grow in maturity, and recommit yourself to achieving your full potential in the future.

CHAPTER 8

The Practise of Gratitude and Mindfulness, which is Chapter 8
The strong practice of thankfulness and mindfulness may considerably improve one's general well-being and the level of pleasure one derives from life if one cultivates these practices. They entail focusing on the here and now, enjoying the good things in your life, and cultivating a greater feeling of thankfulness for the things you already possess.

The following are some ways in which you might develop an attitude of appreciation and mindfulness:

1. have a thankfulness notebook That You Update Daily One of the best habits you can get into is to have a thankfulness notebook that you update daily. It might be anything as straightforward as a breathtaking sunset, a kind act from a close friend, or a personal achievement.

2. Engage in Mindfulness Meditation: Make sure you schedule time in your schedule every day to engage in mindfulness meditation. Pay attention to the sensations in your body, your breath, or the noises in the environment. This practice will help you remain centered and in the here and now.

3. Appreciate the Little Things: It's important to pay attention to the little pleasures and delights that occur throughout your day. Learning to take pleasure in life's little pleasures might help one feel more fulfilled and happy.

4. Practice mindful eating by savoring each mouthful and paying attention to the flavor, texture, and scent of your meal. This is the fourth step in the mindful eating process. This strategy allows you to get the most out of each meal while minimizing the risk of overindulging.

5. Gratitude Walks: When you go for a walk or engage in other activities outside, take some time to think about the things in nature and your environment for which you are thankful.

6. Put Your Attention on Positive Affirmations To build appreciation and mindfulness, you should use positive affirmations. Repeat affirmations that will help you develop a deeper sense of gratitude and presence at the moment.

7. Carry Out Acts of Compassion and Service to Others Carry out acts of compassion and service to other people. Giving back to the community may amplify feelings of gratitude and increase mindfulness.

8. Reduce Your Involvement in Multiple Tasks Try to limit the number of things you have going on at once and focus all of your concentration on a single endeavor at a time. Because of this, you can enjoy each moment to its fullest extent.

9. Engage in Mindful pauses Throughout the Day: Throughout the day, engage in mindful pauses in which you stop, deep breathe, and bring your attention back to the here and now.

10. Show people that you are glad for their presence or acts by expressing your appreciation to them and letting them know that you are thankful for them. Thankfulness is a powerful tool for strengthening relationships with people.

11. Develop a nonjudgmental awareness of your thoughts and feelings by engaging in the practice of nonjudgmental awareness. Just accept things as they are, without judgment or attachment.

12. *Practice mindful breathing by taking several deep breaths and focusing your attention on each inhalation and exhalation as you do so. This may be helpful when you are feeling anxious or overwhelmed.*

13. *Maintain complete Presence During talks It is important to maintain complete presence when having talks with other people. Pay close attention and avoid being distracted as you do so.*

14. *Forgive and let go of grudges; this is the fourteenth and last step in letting go of grudges. Keeping a grudge might make it more difficult to practice gratitude and mindfulness.*

15. Reflect on three things that occurred during the day for which you are glad before going to bed. This is the gratitude reflection for number 15. This kind of introspection before bedtime might help promote a more optimistic frame of mind.

The road to cultivating appreciation and mindfulness needs regular practice and increased awareness of oneself. As you continue to engage in these practices, you will notice that you become more sensitive to the beauty and plenty that already exists in your life, which will ultimately result in increased happiness, satisfaction, and general well-being.

The Crucial Part That Gratitude Plays in Molding Your Mentality

Being appreciative, demonstrating appreciation for a gift, or paying a favor forward are all examples of the emotion known as thankfulness. The majority of people have the goal of finding happiness in their lives, but some people simply can't seem to figure out how to get there. They have the mindset that "If only this would happen, then I'd finally be happy." Sadly, they have things in the wrong order. The pursuit of happiness is often the first step. Being appreciative is the most important step towards achieving pleasure in this now.

People hunt for professions that will make them happy or people who will make them happy, but the fact is, and maybe the secret to happiness is, that we should be happy first, both before and throughout the road towards our objectives as well as after we have achieved them. You know, researchers recently concluded that happy individuals are first and foremost content with the circumstances in which they find themselves. They are not dependent on anybody or anything to "make" them happy; rather, they just are. Consequently, people who hold the notion that they will be joyful when a certain event occurs are often not particularly happy at all when that event occurs. Because after a person accomplishes one goal, they almost always move on to another, loftier, and often more challenging one, and they seldom give themselves enough time to linger on the bliss they promised themselves.

The fact that expressing thanks takes so little of our time is perhaps the aspect of thankfulness that fascinates us the most. Just focusing on two or three things that you are thankful for immediately before going to bed may boost your mood and provide you additional opportunities to be grateful for in the future, according to research conducted by scientists. Let us go into further detail.

The following is a list of the five marvels of gratitude:

Being grateful brings more of what it is that we are thankful for into our lives. Natasha, one of my close friends, compares the cosmos to Google. If you go to Google and put in "don't show me red shoes," the search engine will still display you a selection of red footwear. You have to train yourself to concentrate on the things for which you are thankful, and there is no better way to do this than to make a list of all the things for which you are glad. According to the global law of attraction, we bring to ourselves more of what we focus our attention on. Therefore, practicing gratitude every day makes perfect sense. You develop a conscious awareness of your blessings, seeing what it is that you are grateful for clearly in your mind, feeling glad for it, and as a result, attracting more of those things into your life, similar to how a Google search works.

Gratitude is a powerful antidote to pessimism. You may lessen the amount of negativity in your life by making it a daily practice to come up with three new things for which you are thankful. This will train your mind to turn towards the positive rather than concentrating on the bad. Keeping your mind on the things for which you are thankful can keep you cheerful, upbeat, and optimistic. Practicing thankfulness forces you to think outside of the box and opens fresh perspectives whenever you are confronted with a difficulty. Those that engage in this activity tend to have a more optimistic outlook because they are better able to notice the many advantages and chances that are available to them, rather than focusing primarily on the obstacles that stand in their way.

Being grateful helps us become better at finding solutions to problems, which in turn helps us learn. We all have things that need to be fixed, problems that need to be solved, and barriers that need to be overcome. As we go through life, the obstacles that stand in our way may take some careful consideration and unwavering resolve. Being appreciative, and expressing thanks for what one currently has, opens up one's mind to new opportunities and new relationships. The attitude of gratitude prepares our minds for transformation. Instead of feeling like we are at a standstill, we are provided with a viewpoint that emphasizes growth and possibility. We are aware of the resources and capabilities we currently possess, and we are confident in our ability to prevail. When we shift our attention from the issue at hand to the potential solutions, we open ourselves up to new possibilities. Appreciative people are open to new experiences and find that they are much more thankful when they get the chance to gain new knowledge.

A grateful attitude makes for better partnerships. When we were younger, we were often reminded to say "thank you." We were urged to make it a routine by our parents and other adults, who often questioned us with, "What do you say?" Our response was a more drawn-out version of "thank you." Prayer and grace before meals were traditions that we upheld in our household. By demonstrating gratitude towards our parents, God, and the other adults in our lives, we were able to strengthen the relationships we had as children with these important figures. How does it make you feel to know that other people value you? What kind of an effect does this appreciation have on any of the relationships in your life? No doubt demonstrating or expressing appreciation to another person for the positive influence they have had on your life has a multiplicative effect on all parties involved. When you express gratitude to your employees and coworkers, you let them know that you recognize the value they bring to the team. People who believe they are appreciated work harder to contribute even more value to the group.

Being grateful improves our physical health. In addition, according to scientific research, we now know that cultivating an "attitude of gratitude" is another step towards leading a happier and healthier life. When we practice gratitude, it makes us happy, and when we are happier, our bodies and minds are inherently healthier on a molecular level. A long life, good health, abundant wealth, and a prosperous future are all possible outcomes that can be attributed to an attitude of gratitude and thanksgiving.

Gratitude is not just a feeling; it's also an attitude, a routine, and a choice.

When you intentionally express gratitude for the experiences and people you already have in your life, you will find that you attract even more reasons to be grateful for the things and people in your life. One can choose to be happy and grateful or one can train oneself to have that mindset. It comes down to a choice. You are the one who must make the choice to be grateful and then actively search for the reasons why. Immediately make that decision, and then encourage others to do the same. Thanksgiving is a wonderful holiday to celebrate.

Engaging in Mindfulness Practices to Maintain Presence and Grounding

In this fast-paced and sometimes chaotic world that we live in, one of the most effective ways to maintain the presence of mind and a sense of one's grounding is to engage in the practice of mindfulness. The practice of mindfulness entails bringing one's attention to the here and now while maintaining an attitude of non-judgmental awareness. By growing mindfulness, you may decrease stress, increase attention, and boost your general well-being.

Here are some practical techniques to cultivate mindfulness and remain present and grounded:

1. Mindful Breathing: Take a few minutes each day to concentrate on your breath. Pay attention to the

feeling of the breath entering and exiting your body. If your mind wanders, softly bring your concentration back to the breath.

2. Body Scan: Practice a body scan meditation when you deliberately concentrate on various regions of your body, recognizing any feelings without judgment.

3. Mindful Eating: Slow down and appreciate each mouthful throughout meals. Pay attention to the flavor, texture, and scent of your meal.

4. Mindful Walking: Take a stroll outdoors and observe the feeling of each stride. Feel the earth under your feet and the movement of your body.

5. Be Present in Activities: Whatever you're doing, whether it's cleaning dishes, working, or spending time with loved ones, be present in the moment.

6. Mindful Observation: Take a few minutes to study your surroundings without judgment. Notice the colors, shapes, and textures around you.

7. Mindful Listening: When someone is speaking to you, give them your entire attention. Listen intently and without interrupting.

8. Let Go of Distractions When you become aware of a distraction, notice it without passing judgment on it and then return your attention to the here and now in a calm and collected manner.

9. *Mindful Gratitude:* To cultivate an attitude of gratitude, you should think about the things in your life for which you are grateful.

10. Observe your thoughts and feelings without assigning them any positive or negative connotations as you practice nonjudgmental awareness. Simply take note of them as they pass through the scene.

11. *Mindful Consumption of Media:* Pay attention to how you take in information and entertainment from various sources. Reduce the amount of mindless scrolling you do and focus instead on selecting stuff that is

uplifting and enriching to your well-being.

12. Practice Mindful Breathing During Times of Stress When you find yourself in a stressful situation or feeling overwhelmed, try taking a few long, slow breaths to help calm your nervous system.

13. Incorporate Mindful Moments Into Your Day Stop what you're doing periodically during the day and take a few conscious breaths to bring your attention and concentration back to the present.

14. Pay Attention to the Road, Your Surroundings, and Your Activities Behind the Wheel When you are behind the wheel, you should pay attention to the road, your surroundings, and your activities.

15. To engage with technology mindfully, schedule certain periods during which you will use it and work on being completely present during those times.

When one engages in the practice of mindfulness, the focus is not on attaining a level of perfection but rather on developing a non-judgmental awareness of the here and now. It is natural for your thoughts to stray from time to time; the important thing is to gently bring your focus back to the present anytime you become aware that your mind has wandered. Regular practice of mindfulness may result in increased feelings of calm and clarity, as well as a more profound sense of connectedness with both oneself and the world around them.

Discovering Happiness Along the Way and Honoring Important Milestones

Life is a journey, and each day we make progress toward realizing our ambitions and achieving our objectives. However, we often fail to enjoy the trip itself because we are so preoccupied with the goal that we have set for ourselves. Honoring the path you've traveled is an important component of leading a life that is rewarding. It enables you to have gratitude for the progress you've made and to take pleasure in the *seemingly little successes you achieve along the path.*

To begin, appreciating the accomplishments along the way might help you maintain your motivation. It's easy to lose track of how far you've come when your main concentration is on the destination you're trying to reach. Celebrating your journey allows you to recognize your successes and experience the pride that comes from your hard work. This feeling of accomplishment may serve as a motivating factor, allowing you to keep working towards the objectives you set for yourself.

Second, remembering and appreciating where you've been helps you become more resilient. The roller coaster ride that is life is best navigated by taking time to acknowledge and appreciate even the little victories along the way. Celebrating your journey may help you create the resilience you need to push through obstacles and keep going ahead in life. This is why it is so important to do so.

The third benefit of enjoying your path is that it enables you to discover delight in the here and now. Many times, we are so intent on what it is that we want to accomplish that we fail to appreciate what we have right now. Even if you haven't arrived at your desired destination yet, finding pleasure in the process may be facilitated by celebrating your trip. It enables you to take pleasure in the trip itself, rather than focusing only on the end goal.

So, how exactly can you commemorate this incredible journey? Here are some concepts to consider:

Think about how far you've come. Spend some time reflecting on the beginning of this journey and how far you've gone since then. Record your successes and pat yourself on the back for them.

Don't keep your successes to yourself; tell others about them. No rule says celebrating your journey has to be something you do on your own. Tell your loved ones and close friends about your successes so that they may continue to root for you and encourage you.

Be kind to yourself. Take some time out of your busy schedule to do something pleasant for yourself, whether it be a delicious dinner, a day at a spa, or a brand-new book.

Enjoy even the little victories. Do not put off celebrating important accomplishments until they have been reached. Rejoice in the accomplishment of less significant goals along the road, such as successfully finishing challenging work or acquiring a new ability.

Spend some time focusing on appreciating the here and now.

Remember to give yourself some space and focus on the here and now every once in a while. Spend your time engaging in activities that bring you delight, surround yourself with positive people, and learn to discover pleasure in the process.